WORLD ENGLISH Intro

THIRD EDITION

Real People • Real Places • Real Language

John Hughes, Author

Martin Milner, Author

NATIONAL
GEOGRAPHIC
LEARNING

Australia · Brazil · Mexico · Singapore · United Kingdom · United States

National Geographic Learning,
a Cengage Company

World English Level Intro: Real People, Real Places, Real Language, Third Edition
John Hughes and Martin Milner

Publisher: Sherrise Roehr

Executive Editor: Sarah Kenney

Senior Development Editor: Brenden Layte

Media Researcher: Leila Hishmeh

Senior Technology Product Manager:
  Lauren Krolick

Director of Global Marketing: Ian Martin

Senior Product Marketing Manager:
  Caitlin Thomas

Heads of Regional Marketing:
  Charlotte Ellis (Europe, Middle East, and Africa)
  Kiel Hamm (Asia)
  Irina Pereyra (Latin America)

Production Manager: Daisy Sosa

Manufacturing Planner: Mary Beth Hennebury

Art Director: Brenda Carmichael

Operations Support: Hayley Chwazik-Gee

Cover Image: Trey Ratcliff

Compositor: MPS Limited

For permission to use material from this text or product,
submit all requests online at **cengage.com/permissions**
Further permissions questions can be emailed to
permissionrequest@cengage.com

World English 1 ISBN: 978-0-357-11366-0
World English 1 + MyWorldEnglishOnline ISBN: 978-0-357-13019-3

National Geographic Learning
200 Pier 4 Boulevard
Boston, MA 02210
USA

Locate your local office at **international.cengage.com/region**

Visit National Geographic Learning online at **ELTNGL.com**
Visit our corporate website at www.cengage.com

Printed in Mexico
Print Number: 01   Print Year: 2019

Thank you to the educators who provided invaluable feedback during the development of the third edition of the *World English* series:

AMERICAS

Brazil

Gabriely Billordo, Berlitz, Porto Alegre
Bruna Caltabiano, Caltabiano Idiomas, Sao Paulo
Sophia de Carvalho, Inglês Express, Belo Horizonte
Renata Coelho, 2b English for you, Florianopolis
Rebecca Ashley Hibas, Inglês Express, Belo Horizonte
Cristina Kobashi, Cultivar Escola de Idiomas, Guaratinguetá
Silvia Teles Barbosa, Colégio Cândido Portinari, Salvador

Chile

Jorge Cuevas, Universidad Santo Tomás, Los Angeles

Colombia

Ruben Cano, UPB University, Medellin
Javier Vega, Fundación Universitaria de Popayán, Popayán

Costa Rica

Jonathan Acuña, Centro Cultural Costarricense Americano, San José
Lilly Sevilla, Centro Cultural Costarricense Americano, San José

Mexico

José Aguirre, Instituto Tecnológico Superior de Irapuato, Salamanca
Alejandro Alvarado Cupil, Instituto Tecnológico de Minatitlán, Minatitlán
Jhosellin Ángeles, ITSOEH, Mixquiahuala de Juárez, Hidalgo
René Bautista, BUAP, Puebla
Imelda Félix, Colegio Cervantes Costa Rica, Guadalajara
Isabel Fernández, Universidad Autónoma de Aguascalientes, Aguascalientes
Andrés Garcia, FES Aragón (UNAM), Mexico City
Jéssica Garcia, Colegio Cultural, Puebla
Lázaro Garcia, Tecnológico de Toluca, Metepec
Fernando Gómez, Universidad Tecnológica Jalisco, Guadalajara
Alma Gopar, FES Zaragoza (UNAM), Mexico City
Inés Gutiérrez, University of Colima, Colima
Jesús Chávez Hernández, Universidad Aeronáutica en Querétaro, Colón
Cristina Méndez, Instituto Tecnológico Superior de Irapuato, Irapuato
Elena Mioto, UNIVA, Guadalajara
Rubén Mauricio Muñoz Morales, Universidad Santo Tomás, Villavicencio
María Rodríguez, Universidad Aeronáutica en Querétaro, Colón
Ana Lilia Terrazas, ICO, Puebla

United States

Amy Fouts, Face to Face Learning Center, Doral, FL
Virginia Jorge, UCEDA International, New Brunswick, NJ
Richard McDorman, Language On, Miami, FL
Sarah Mikulski, Harper College, Palatine, IL
Rachel Scheiner, Seattle Central College, Seattle, WA
Pamela Smart-Smith, Virginia Tech Language and Culture Institute, Blacksburg, VA
Marcie Stone, American English College, Rowland Heights, CA
Colin Ward, Lone Star College-North Harris, Houston, TX
Marla Yoshida, University of California Irvine, CA

ASIA

Nazarul Azali, UiTM Cawangan Melaka, Alor Gajah
Steven Bretherick, Tohoku Fukushi University, Sendai
Sam Bruce, Soka University, Hachioji
Karen Cline-Katayama, Hokusei Gakuen University and Tokai University, Sapporo
Tom David, Japan College of Foreign Languages, Tokyo
Johnny Eckstein, Soka University, Hachioji
Meg Ellis, Kyoto Tachibana University, Kyoto
Thomas Goetz, Hokusei Gakuen University, Sapporo
Katsuko Hirai, Matsuyama University, Matsuyama
Paul Horness, Soka University, Hachioji
David Kluge, Nanzan University, Nagoya
Stephen Lambacher, Aoyama Gakuin University, Tokyo
Yi-An Lin, National Taipei University of Business, Taipei
Kerry McCatty, Soka University, Hachioji
Gregg McNabb, Shizuoka Institute of Technology, Shizuoka
Collin Mehmet, Matsumoto University, Matsumoto City
Sean Mehmet, Shinshu University, Matsumoto
Lin Mingying, Soka University, Hachioji
Erika Nakatsuka, Soka University, Hachioji
Seiko Oguri, Chubu University, Nagoya
Thomas Nishikawa, Ritsumeikan University, Kyoto
Sean Otani, Tottori University, Tottori
Daniel Paller, Kinjo Gakuin University, Nagoya
Tomomi Sasaki, Ibaraki University, Mito
Mark Shrosbree, Tokai University, Hiratsuka
Brent Simmons, Aichi Gakuin University, Nagoya
Mikiko Sudo, Soka University, Hachioji
Monika Szirmai, Hiroshima International University, Hiroshima
Matthew Taylor, Kinjo Gakuin University, Nagoya
James Thomas, Kokusai Junior College, Tokyo
Asca Tsushima, Soka University, Hachioji
Hui Chun Yu, Macau University of Science and Technology, Macau

Unit	Unit Goals	Grammar	Vocabulary
1 Friends and Family Page 2	• Meet and Introduce People • Spell Names and Words • Describe People • Present Your Family • Give Personal Information	Present Tense of *be* *I'm Kim. / They're Maria and Lola.* *Be* + Adjective *They're young. Is John single?* Questions with *be* and Short Answers ***Are** you married?* *Yes, I **am** / No, I'm **not**.*	Greetings and Introductions Names and Spelling Adjectives to Describe People Family Members
2 Jobs around the World Page 16	• Identify Jobs • Ask about Jobs • Talk about Cities and Countries • Compare Jobs • Interview People	Negative Present of *be*; Indefinite Articles *He **isn't** a doctor. Pat**'s an** artist.* *Be* + Adjective + Noun *Russia **is a big country**.*	Jobs Numbers Cities, Countries, and Continents
3 Houses and Apartments Page 30	• Talk about Rooms • Compare Houses • Say Where Objects Are • Give Your Opinion • Describe Your Home	*There is / There are*; Singular and Plural Nouns ***There are** three bedrooms.* ***Is there** a garage?* Prepositions of Place: *in, on, under, next to, between* *Your magazine is **under** your bag.*	Places in a Home Furniture and Household Objects
4 Possessions Page 44	• Ask about Possessions • Present a Special Object • Talk about What You Have • Identify Similarities and Differences • Thank Someone for a Present	Demonstratives *Are **these** your books? **That** is not your bag.* Possession *It's **Jim's** bag.* *Have, Has* *She **has** a phone.*	Personal Possessions Opinion Adjectives
5 Daily Activities Page 58	• Tell Time • Compare People's Daily Routines • Talk about Activities at Work and School • Present a Report • Give Advice and Instructions	Simple Present *They **get up** at 7 o'clock.* Simple Present Questions and Answers ***Do** you **go** to class every day? Yes, I **do**.* Adverbs of Frequency: *always, sometimes, never* *I **never** answer the phone.* Imperatives	Daily Activities Telling Time Work and School Activities Time Expressions
6 Getting Around Page 72	• Ask For and Give Directions • Create a Tour • Compare Types of Transportation • Plan a Bicycle Day • Give Advice to Travelers	Prepositions of Place and Movement ***Turn** left and **walk** for two blocks.* *The hotel is **across from** the park.* *Go **up** the stairs.* *Have to* *She **has to** change buses.*	Places Around a Town or City Directions Ground Transportation

Listening	Speaking and Pronunciation	Reading	Writing	Video Journal
Listening for General Understanding and Specific Information: Conversations around School	Meeting People and Introducing Yourself Asking and Answering Questions about Personal Information The Alphabet	A Family of Explorers	Filling Out Personal Information Capital Letters	**My Name** In this video from National Geographic Learning, author Taiye Selasi talks about her name, what it means, and how it came to be.
Focused Listening and Listening for Specific Information: A Conversation about the Jobs of Two National Geographic Explorers	Asking about Jobs Asking For and Giving Personal Information Interviewing a Classmate Describing Places Around the World Numbers	Women at Work	Writing and Performing an Interview Punctuation Marks	**A Contact Job** In this video from National Geographic, contact juggler Okotanpe shows off his skills in Tokyo, Japan.
Listening for General Understanding and Specific Details: People Talking about Their Homes	Describing Your Home Saying Where Things Are Syllables and Stressed Syllables	Home Sweet Home?	Writing a Description of Your Home *and*	**A Day in the Life of a Lighthouse Keeper** This video from the National Geographic Short Film Showcase follows a day in the life of a lighthouse keeper in Uruguay.
Listening for Specific Information: A Conversation about a Surprising Art Project	Talking about Personal Possessions Talking about Giving Gifts Talking about a Special Object /i/ and /ɪ/ Sounds	My Room	Short Emails and Messages	**Tyler Bikes Across America** This video shows bicyclist and photographer Tyler Metcalfe's journey across the United States—on his bike.
Listening for General Understanding and Specific Details: A Podcast about the Day of a "Super Commuter"	Asking and Answering Questions about Work or School Activities and Daily Routines Discussing and Giving Advice Falling Intonation on Statements and Information Questions	Screen Time	Writing a To-Do List Lists and Notes	**Around the World in 24 Hours** This video from National Geographic Learning goes on a journey to see what people are doing around the world at different times of day.
Listening for Specific Information: A Walking Tour of Paraty, Brazil	Asking For and Giving Directions Quizzing Classmates about Your City or Country *Yes / No* Questions and Short Answers	A City that Bans Cars on Sundays	Writing a Reply to a Message Describing What to Do in Your City Connectors (*and*, *but*, *because*)	***Star Wars* on the Subway** This video features Improv Everywhere—a group of performers who try to make people laugh and have fun in public places—performing the movie *Star Wars* ... on the subway.

Unit	Unit Goals	Grammar	Vocabulary
7 Free Time Page 86	• Identify Activities Happening Now • Make a Phone Call • Talk about Abilities • Explain How to Play Something • Interview People	Present Continuous *I'm **not watching** TV. I'm **reading**.* *Can* for Ability *He **can't** play the guitar. He **can** sing.*	Pastimes Sports
8 Clothes Page 100	• Ask about Clothes • Buy Clothes • Express Likes and Dislikes • Talk about Personal Qualities • Describe Your Favorites	*Can / Could* for Polite Requests ***Can** I try on these shoes?* Object Pronouns *I love **them**! / She hates **it**.*	Colors Clothes Likes and Dislikes
9 Food Page 114	• Order a Meal • Plan a Party • Describe Your Diet • Solve a Problem • Explain How To Do Something	*Some* and *Any* *There's **some** ice cream in the fridge.* Count and Non-count Nouns; *How much / How many* ***How many** oranges do we need?* ***How much** chocolate do we have?*	Food Meals Containers Quantities Food Groups
10 Health Page 128	• Identify Parts of the Body and Say How You Feel • Ask about Health Problems • Give Advice on Health Remedies • Explain a Process • Describe Healthy Living	Review of Simple Present *My back **hurts**.* *Feel, Look* + Adjective *John **looks** terrible. I **feel** sick.* *Should* (for advice) *You **should** take an aspirin.*	Parts of the Body Common Illnesses and Health Problems Remedies
11 Making Plans Page 142	• Plan Special Days • Describe a National Holiday • Make Life Plans • Compare Festivals • Invite People	*Be going to* *What **are** you **going to** do?* *We **are going to** have a party.* *Would like to* for Wishes *I **would like to** be a doctor.*	Special Days and Plans Months of the Year Holidays Professions
12 On the Move Page 156	• Talk about Your Past • Ask about the Past • Describe a Vacation • Compare the Past and Present • Give Biographical Information	Simple Past *We **went** to the mountains.* *He **moved** from San Francisco to New York.* Simple Past Questions ***Was** he born in 2001?* *Where **did** you live?*	Verbs + Prepositions of Movement Going on Vacation

Listening	Speaking and Pronunciation	Reading	Writing	Video Journal
Listening for Specific Information: Telephone Conversations in Different Contexts	Having a Phone Conversation Asking and Answering Questions to Fill Out an Application Form and Do a Job Interview Connected Speech	Hybrid Sports	Writing a Job Application Form Question Forms (simple present, present continuous, questions with *can*)	**Danny's Challenge** This video from National Geographic shows stunt cyclist Danny MacAskill as he does tricks on the streets of Edinburgh, Scotland.
Listening for Specific Details: Listening to People Shopping for Clothes	Describing Clothes Shopping Describing Likes and Dislikes Playing a Game about Your Favorite Things *Could you*	What Does the Color of Your Clothes Say about You?	Writing about Favorites Paragraphs	**A Dress with a Story** This video from National Geographic's Short Film Showcase shows a group of women in Sardinia, Italy, who wear and work on one dress for their entire lives.
Listening for Specific Details: Conversation to Confirm a Shopping List for a Party	Planning a Party Talking about Your Diet Discussing a "How To" List *And*	Food Waste	Writing a "How To" List Giving Examples	**Berry Road Trip** This video from National Geographic shows the journey that strawberries take from farm to customer, and the resources that this journey requires.
Listening for General Understanding and Specific Details: Describing Symptoms to a Doctor	Describing Symptoms and Illnesses Giving Advice Talking about How to Live a Long and Healthy Life Sound and Spelling	A Life-Saving Delivery	Writing a Paragraph about Mental Health Sequencing and Adding Information	**What Makes You Happy?** This video from National Geographic shows what makes people happy around the world and spotlights three of the happiest countries: Costa Rica, Denmark, and Singapore.
Listening for General Understanding and Specific Details: Holiday Traditions	Talking about Celebrating Holidays Talking about Life Plans Inviting People to Events *Be going to* (Reduced Form)	Spring Festivals	Writing an Invitation More Formal and Less Formal Writing	**Catching a Hummingbird** This video from National Geographic follows photographer Anand Varma as he plans a project to film a hummingbird, and then shows the beautiful result.
Listening for General Understanding and Specific Details: An Interview with Archaeologist Chris Thornton	Describing a Vacation Giving Biographical Information *-ed* Endings	Humans and Animals on the Move	Writing a Biography Time Expressions and Linking Words	**Leaving Antarctica** In this video from National Geographic, a man who was born in Antarctica talks about how much it has changed and discusses his reasons for leaving.

Friends and Family

Around the world, people
have friends and family.
They are young and old,
and they come from
different places.

Look at the photos and answer the questions.

1 Are these people young or old?

2 Who is young in your family? Who is old?

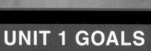

UNIT 1 GOALS

A. Meet and Introduce People

B. Spell Names and Words

C. Describe People

D. Present Your Family

E. Give Personal Information

3

A **GOAL** Meet and Introduce People

Vocabulary

A 🎧 2 Listen and repeat.

Greetings

B Greet your classmates informally.

C Greet your teacher formally.

D 🎧 3 Listen and repeat.

Introductions

Informal greetings and responses

Hi! How's it going?
  Great! | Fine. | OK.

Formal greetings and responses

Good morning | afternoon | evening.
How are you?
  Fine, | I'm well, thank you.

E In pairs, write and practice a formal conversation using these words.

A: Hello / name's *Hello, my name's ...* _____

B: Nice / meet / My name's _____

A: Nice / meet / too _____

F In groups of three, practice an informal conversation using these words.

A: Hi / This / friend   **B:** Hello / name's   **C:** Hi

Grammar

Present Tense of *be*		
Subject Pronoun	*Be*	
I	**am**	
You	**are**	Kim.
He / She	**is**	
We	**are**	Lucas and Ed.
They	**are**	Maria and Claudia.

Contractions with *be*
I**'m**
you**'re**
he**'s** / she**'s**
we**'re**
they**'re**

Possessive Adjectives	
My	name is Mario.
Your	name is Rachel.
His	name is Robert.
Her	name is May.
Their	names are Ben and Dan.

G Write the correct form of the verb *be.*

1. Their names ___are___ Julie and Les.
2. My name _____ Victor.
3. I _____ Said.
4. We _____ Rigo and Rosana.
5. His name _____ Arata.
6. Your name _____ Yan-Ching.

H Unscramble the sentences.

1. Ron. / name / My / is   My name is Ron. _____
2. Leila. / is / name / Her   _____
3. is / name / Mr. Aoki. / His   _____
4. Chen. / Their / Marcos / names / are / and / _____

I 🎧 4   Listen to the conversation. Which phrases are informal? Which are formal?

Donna: Hi, Nick. How's it going?

Nick: Great! And you?

Donna: Fine.

Nick: Donna, this is my friend, Hiroshi.

Donna: Nice to meet you, Hiroshi.

Hiroshi: Nice to meet you, too, Donna.

J Practice the conversation in groups of three.

K Practice the conversation again with your own names.

✓ GOAL CHECK   Meet and Introduce People

1. In pairs, meet each other and introduce yourselves.
2. Stand up. Walk around and meet another pair. Introduce your partner.

(Hi! How are you?)   (Fine, thanks.)   (Hello. My name's ...)   (This is ...)   (Nice to meet you.)

GOAL Spell Names and Words

Listening

A 🎧 5 Listen to three conversations. Match the conversation (1–3) to the place (a–c).

a. In a classroom _____

b. In an office _____

c. At a university _____

B 🎧 5 Complete the questions with the words below. Then listen again and check.

> first   last name   spell   word   you   your

REAL LANGUAGE

Names

first name given name

last name surname / family name

Mr. a man (single or married)

Ms. a woman (single or married)

Mrs. a woman (married)

Miss a woman (single)

1. What's your _____?

2. How do you _____ that?

3. What's the English _____ for this?

4. Can _____ repeat that?

5. What's your _____ name?

6. How do I spell _____ name?

C 🎧 5 Listen again. Spell the names and word from the conversation.

1. R O _ R I _ U E _

2. T _ B _ E

3. L I _ J U _

The entrance of the University of Southern Denmark in Kolding, Denmark

PRONUNCIATION: The Alphabet

6 Listen and repeat the letters of the alphabet.

A B C D E F G H I J K L M N O P Q R S T U V W X Y Z

D **7** Listen to and read the conversation.

Hussein: How do I spell your name?
Tim: T-I-M.
Hussein: T-I-N?
Tim: No, T-I-M. That's *T* as in teacher. *I* as in Italy. *M* as in man.
Hussein: Thanks.
Tim: You're welcome.

SPEAKING STRATEGY

For words that are hard to spell, you can use words and names of places to be clear. *A as in apple, B as in Brazil, C as in cat.*

E In pairs, practice the conversation with your own names.

Communication

F Answer the questions in the first column of the table for yourself. Write your answers in the *Me* column.

	Me	Classmate 1	Classmate 2
What's your first name?			
What's your last name?			
What's your favorite English word?			

G In groups of three, take turns asking the questions. Spell your names and favorite words.

(What's your ... ?) (My first name is ...) (How do you spell that?) (Can you repeat that?)

GOAL CHECK Spell Names and Words

In pairs, tell your partner about the two classmates in **G**. Say and spell their names and favorite words.

(His first name is ...) (Her favorite word is ...) (You spell it F-R-I-E-N-D.)

GOAL Describe People

Language Expansion: Adjectives

A Write the correct word(s) under the photos.

| attractive | married / single | old / young | tall / average / short |

1. _____ 2. _____ 3. _____ 4. _____

B Describe yourself. Underline the correct adjectives.

1. I am *old / young* and I'm *single / married*.
2. I'm *short / average height / tall* with *short / long* hair.

Grammar

Be + Adjective					
Subject + *be* + Adjective					
I	**am**	young.	Emily	**is**	young and short.
You	**are**	tall and handsome.	We	**are**	married.
John	**is**	old with gray hair.	They	**are**	tall with curly, black hair.

C In pairs, take turns to describe yourselves. Then describe your classmates.

Use the verb *be* + adjectives and the word *with* + *long / short / curly* to describe hair.

> I am young with long, red hair.

> David is tall and handsome.

> She's young and single with short, blond hair.

D Describe a student to the class. The class guesses the student.

> He's tall with short, brown hair.

 It's Miguel.

 Correct!

WORD FOCUS

He's **attractive**. =
    He's **handsome**.
She's **attractive**. =
    She's **beautiful**.

long black hair

short gray hair

curly red hair

long blond hair

short brown hair

Questions with *be*			Short Answers		
Are	you	married?	Yes, I **am**.		No, I**'m not**.
Is	he / she	tall?	Yes, he / she **is**.		No, he / she **isn't**. No, he**'s** / she**'s not**.
Are	they	single?	Yes, they **are**.		No, they**'re not**. No, they **aren't**.

E Match the questions to the answers.

1. Is your friend tall? _____
2. Is Emma tall? _____
3. Are you single? _____
4. Are your teachers old? _____

a. Yes, she is.
b. No, he isn't. He's short.
c. No, they're not. They're young.
d. Yes, I am.

F Fill in the blanks with a question or an answer.

1. **Q:** Is she short _____?
   A: No, she isn't. She's tall.

2. **Q:** _____?
   A: No, she isn't. She is short with blond hair.

3. **Q:** Is Alicia attractive?
   A: _____.

4. **Q:** _____?
   A: Yes, she is. Her husband's name is Marco.

Conversation

G 🎧 8 Listen to the conversation. Then practice the conversation in pairs.

Ana: Who's this in the photo?
Carol: It's a friend in my class.
Ana: What's <u>his</u> name?
Carol: <u>Richard</u>.
Ana: <u>He's</u> <u>handsome</u>! Is <u>he</u> married?
Carol: Yes, <u>he</u> is!

H Change the underlined words and make a new conversation.

SPEAKING STRATEGY

Ask about Other People

Who's this?

Who are they?

What's his / her name?

What are their names?

Is he / she ...?

Are they ...?

 GOAL CHECK Describe People

In pairs, write the names or show photos of three people (friends or famous people). Take turns to ask questions about the people and describe them.

GOAL Present Your Family

Reading

A Read the article. Circle **Y** for *yes* or **N** for *no*.

1. Is Emily a teacher?   **Y**   **N**

2. Is Emily from California?   **Y**   **N**

3. Is Mary a scientist and an explorer?   **Y**   **N**

4. Is Dorothy a friend?   **Y**   **N**

5. Is Doctor Nigel Hughes with the family?   **Y**   **N**

6. Is he a scientist and an explorer?   **Y**   **N**

B Match the names to the family tree.

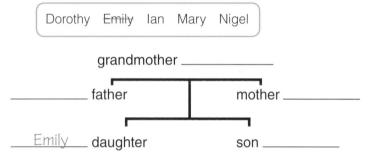

Dorothy   ~~Emily~~   Ian   Mary   Nigel

grandmother _____

_____ father   mother _____

<u>Emily</u> daughter   son _____

C 🎧 10   Listen and repeat the family words. Then answer the questions.

brother	daughter	father	granddaughter
grandfather	grandmother	grandson	husband
mother	sister	son	wife

1. Is each family member a man or a woman? Make two lists in your notebook.

2. Match the opposites. *husband / wife*

D Complete these sentences about Emily's family.

1. Ian is Emily's _____.

2. Mary is Nigel's _____.

3. Dorothy is Mary's _____.

4. Emily is Dorothy's _____.

✓ GOAL CHECK

1. Draw and label your family tree. Then present your family to a partner.

This is my family.

This is my sister. She's ...

A gecko is next to a fossil of Dickinsonia, one of Earth's first animals, in this photo by Dr. Mary Droser.

Writer and photographer
Taiye Selasi

Jobs around the World

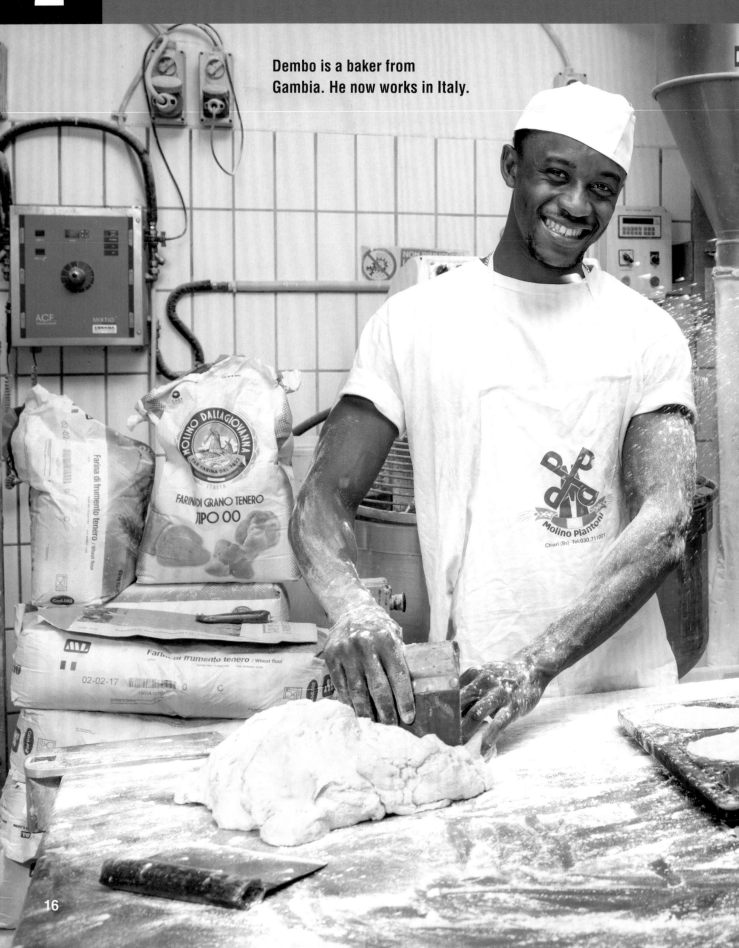

Dembo is a baker from Gambia. He now works in Italy.

Look at the photo and answer the questions.

1 What is Dembo's job? Where is he from?

2 What jobs are popular in your country?

UNIT 2 GOALS

A. Identify Jobs

B. Ask about Jobs

C. Talk about Cities and Countries

D. Compare Jobs

E. Interview People

GOAL Identify Jobs

Vocabulary

A 🎧 11 What are the jobs? Listen and label the photos with words from the box.

> architect   artist   banker   chef   doctor   ~~engineer~~   taxi driver   teacher

1. Jane: _engineer_

2. Eun: _____

3. Oscar: _____

4. Dae-Jung: _____

5. Jim: _____

6. Hannah: _____

7. Harvey: _____

8. Sofia: _____

WORD FOCUS

inside in a building
outside not in a building
*I work **in an office**.* = inside
*I work **in a park**.* = outside

B Which job(s) in **A** is / are...

1. in a car? _a taxi driver_
2. in a school? _____
3. in a hospital? _____
4. in a restaurant? _____
5. in an office? _____
6. outside? _____

Grammar

Negative Present of *be*; Indefinite Articles				
Contractions				Indefinite Articles
I'm not				**a** chef.
You**'re not**	OR	You **aren't**		**an** artist.
He**'s** / She**'s not**		He / She **isn't**		
We**'re** / They**'re not**		We / They **aren't**		artists.
				*We use **a** before a consonant sound. *We use **an** before a vowel sound.

C 🎧 12 Look at the photos in **A**. Listen and fill in the blanks with *is* or *is not*. Then listen and check your answers.

1. Jim ____is____ a taxi driver. He ____is not____ a doctor.

2. Oscar _____ a teacher. He _____ an architect.

3. Sofia _____ an architect. She _____ a doctor.

4. Dae-Jung _____ an engineer. He _____ a chef.

5. Eun _____ a banker. He _____ an artist.

D Fill in the blanks with *a* or *an*. Then look at the people in **A**. Circle **T** for *true* or **F** for *false*.

1. Hannah is __a__ taxi driver.   **T**   **(F)**

2. Jane is ____ engineer.   **T**   **F**

3. Dae-Jung is ____ artist.   **T**   **F**

4. Eun is not ____ doctor.   **T**   **F**

5. Harvey is not ____ architect.   **T**   **F**

E 🎧 13 Listen to the conversation. What are Mary and Laura's new jobs?

REAL LANGUAGE

To show surprise, we can say:
formal ⟷ informal
Really? Amazing! Wow!

Mary: Hi Laura. How's life?

Laura: Fine, thanks. How's your new job?

Mary: Great. I'm <u>a teacher in a school with young children</u>.

Laura: Wow! Is it interesting?

Mary: Yes, very. What about you? Are you still <u>a student</u>?

Laura: No, I'm not. I'm <u>a chef</u> now.

Mary: Really? Where?

Laura: In <u>a restaurant</u> downtown.

F Practice the conversation in pairs. Switch roles and practice it again.

G Change the underlined words and make a new conversation.

✓ **GOAL CHECK** Identify Jobs

Choose a job in **A**. In pairs, ask and answer questions to guess each other's jobs.

> Is it in a hospital?

> Are you a chef?

> Yes, it is. / No, it isn't.

> Yes, I am. / No, I'm not.

GOAL Ask about Jobs

A Look at the photos of two people. What are their jobs?

B 🎧 14 Listen and complete the information.

Name: Joe G_____	Name: Hannah Reyes Morales
Age: _____ years old	Age: _____ years old
Job: _____	Job: _____
Country: Canada	Country: The Philippines
Is his job interesting? Yes / No	Is her job interesting? Yes / No

C Are these jobs interesting to you? Why?

> Photographer is an interesting job. You travel around the world!

D In pairs, take turns reading the numbers in English.

Numbers

0 zero	**10** ten	**20** twenty	**30** thirty
1 one	**11** eleven	**21** twenty-one	**40** forty
2 two	**12** twelve	**22** twenty-two	**50** fifty
3 three	**13** thirteen	**23** twenty-three	**60** sixty
4 four	**14** fourteen	**24** twenty-four	**70** seventy
5 five	**15** fifteen	**25** twenty-five	**80** eighty
6 six	**16** sixteen	**26** twenty-six	**90** ninety
7 seven	**17** seventeen	**27** twenty-seven	**100** one hundred
8 eight	**18** eighteen	**28** twenty-eight	**101** one hundred
9 nine	**19** nineteen	**29** twenty-nine	and one

PRONUNCIATION: Numbers

Listen to the stress in the "teen" (e.g., 13, 14, 15) and "ten" (e.g., 30, 40, 50) forms of a number. For teen numbers, the stress is on the second syllable. For ten numbers, the stress is on the first syllable.

six**teen** – **six**ty

E 🎧 15 Listen and circle what you hear.

1. six   sixteen   sixty

2. four   fourteen   forty

3. three   thirteen   thirty

4. seven   seventeen   seventy

5. eight   eighteen   eighty

F 🎧 16 Listen to this description and write numbers from **E**.

My name's Rafael and I'm (1)_____ years old. I'm a college student. I study science and there are (2)_____ students in my class. I live with my father, my grandmother, and my (3)_____ sisters. My father is a teacher and he's (4)_____ years old. My grandmother is (5)_____ years old. She's a doctor and she still works!

G Complete these sentences about you with a number.

1. I'm _____ years old.

2. I have _____ brothers and sisters.

3. There are _____ students in my class.

H Read your sentences aloud in pairs. Write down your partner's numbers for items 1 and 2.

✓ GOAL CHECK Ask about Jobs

1. Read the questions and write your answers. Then ask two classmates the questions. Write their answers.

	Me	Classmate 1	Classmate 2
What's your name?			
How old are you?			
What's your (dream) job?			
Is it interesting?			

2. Tell a partner about your two classmates above.

Jason is 27 years old and he's a chef.

His job is interesting.

Language Expansion: Cities, Countries, and Continents

A Read about the National Geographic Society. Answer the questions.

1. Is it big or small?
2. Where is its headquarters?
3. Where are the other offices?
4. What jobs are there?

The National Geographic Society

The National Geographic Society is a big organization. Its headquarters is in Washington, DC, the capital city of the United States. There are six more offices on four continents. Lots of people work with the National Geographic Society, such as photographers, explorers, and scientists.

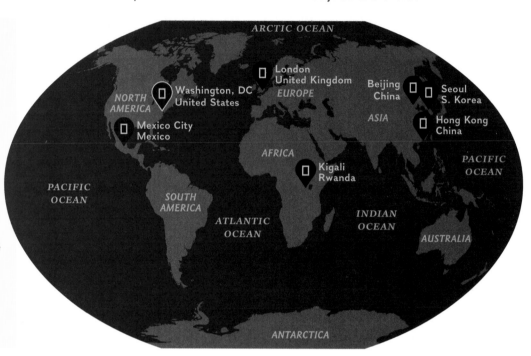

WORD FOCUS

organization a large group of people with one goal
headquarters most important office

B Write the missing city, country, or continent from the map.

1. I'm from the UK and my office is in _____London_____.
2. _____ is in Asia. There are two offices. I'm in the office in Hong Kong.
3. _____ is in the middle of Africa. The capital city is Kigali.
4. We're from _____. Seoul is the capital.
5. _____ is a big city. It's the capital city of Mexico.
6. I'm from South America, but my job is in the US in _____.

C Match the cities to the countries and continents.

Cities	Countries	Continents
São Paulo	Italy	South America
Milan	Brazil	Asia
Jakarta	Indonesia	North America
Vancouver	UAE	Middle East
Dubai	Canada	Europe

D **MY WORLD** What is your town or city? Country? Continent?

Santiago.

Chile ... in South America!

Correct. Two points!

E In small groups, play a game: One student says a city. The others guess the country and continent. You get one point for each. Then another student says a city.

Grammar

Be + Adjective + Noun		
Statement	Question	Answer
Africa **is** a big continent.	**Is** the United Kingdom a big country?	No, it **isn't**. It**'s** a small country.
Paris **is** a beautiful city.	**Is** Apple a big company?	Yes, it **is**.

F Match the question to the answer.

1. Is China a big country? _____

2. Is Rome an interesting city? _____

3. Is Apple a small company? _____

4. Are you at a small college? _____

a. No, it isn't. It's a big company.

b. Yes, it is. There are over 1 billion people.

c. No, I'm not. I'm at Oxford. It's big!

d. Yes, it is. It's also a very old city!

G In pairs, ask and answer questions with these words.

1. Are you from / interesting country?

2. Are / from / big city?

3. Are / from / old city?

4. Are / from / small school?

SPEAKING STRATEGY

Say Where You are From

Where are you from?
 I'm from ...
Are you a (teacher)?
Are you from (China)?
Is it a (town / city / country)?
It's in / near (Egypt / Cairo).

Conversation

H 🎧 17 Where is each person from? Practice the conversation in pairs.

Chris: Hi, I'm Chris. I work with a computer company.

Mohamed: Nice to meet you, Chris. My name's Mohamed.

Chris: Where are you from, Mohamed?

Mohamed: I'm from Egypt.

Chris: Really? Are you from Cairo?

Mohamed: Yes, I am.

Chris: Oh, it's a beautiful city!

Mohamed: Yes, it is. And very old. What about you?

Chris: I'm from Washington, DC. It's a beautiful city, but it isn't old like Cairo.

✓ GOAL CHECK Talk about Cities and Countries

1. Choose a famous person. Write down his or her job, city, country, and continent.

2. Work in pairs. Pretend to be your famous person. Then guess your partner's person.

- Meet the other person and say your person's name and job.

- Ask where the other person is from.

- Ask about their town / city / country.

D GOAL Compare Jobs

Reading

A Look at the photo. Where do you think the woman and her daughter are from?

B Read paragraph 1. Answer the questions.

1. What is Alison's job?
2. Where is she from?
3. Where is her job?
4. Are most of her photographs of men?

C Read paragraph 2. Where do the women ...

1. cook food?
2. make clothes?
3. help people?

D Read paragraph 3. Underline the correct words to complete the sentences.

1. Abau *is* / *isn't* from South Sudan.
2. She *makes* / *buys* clothes.
3. Abau works *at home* / *in a factory*.

✓ GOAL CHECK

1. Compare the jobs in pairs. Check (✓) the words for each job in the table.

	Photographer	Doctor	Farmer
works outside			
travels a lot			
works a lot of hours			
makes something			
helps people			
is interesting			

2. Choose two more jobs and compare them. Use the words in the table.

> A photographer works outside, but a nurse works inside.

> Both are interesting jobs.

WOMEN AT WORK

1   Alison Wright is a photographer. She's from New York, but she works all over the world. She takes photographs for National Geographic and for **humanitarian aid organizations** on different continents— Africa, Asia, South America, and in regions like the Middle East. Lots of her photographs are of women and children.

2   The photo on this page is from a group of photos by Alison. They show "Women at Work." They are photos of women—they cook food or have small businesses at home, and work other jobs like farming, making clothes in factories, or work at hospitals.

3   The photo shows 26-year-old Abau Flora and her daughter. They are from Juba, in South Sudan. Abau has a business—she makes clothes in her home with a sewing machine. Her sewing machine is from an aid organization. With her business, she makes money and helps support her family.

4   The women in the photos Alison takes do many jobs. They all have one thing in common, though: they work hard to create a better future.

humanitarian aid organization an organization that helps people

Communication

A Write five jobs you know. You can use a dictionary to write new jobs (that are not in this unit).

B In pairs, compare your lists. In your opinion, which jobs are interesting? Which jobs are boring?

C Look at the photos of Intan and Henry. Answer the questions in pairs.

1. Where do you think these people are from?
2. What are their jobs?
3. Are they old or young?
4. Are their jobs interesting?
5. Are they inside or outside?

Writing

Use **a period** at the end of a sentence. *I am from Brazil.*
Use **a question mark** at the end of a question. *Are you from Brazil?*
Use **an apostrophe** with contracted forms. *I'm from Brazil.*
Use **a comma** with short answers. *Yes, I am.*
Use **an exclamation mark** to show excitement. *I love my job!*

D Read an interview with Intan. Circle all of the punctuation marks.

A: What's your name?

B: My name's Intan.

A: Where are you from?

B: I'm from Indonesia.

A: What's your job?

B: I'm an ocean diver.

A: Is your job interesting?

B: Yes, it is. But it's also dangerous!

E Read an interview with Henry. Add the punctuation.

A: Whats your name _____

B: My names Henry _____

A: Where are you from _____

B: Im from the US _____

A: Whats your job _____

B: Im a fisherman _____

A: Is your job easy _____

B: No it isnt Its very difficult _____

A: Is it interesting _____

B: Yes it is _____

 GOAL CHECK Interview People

1. Interview a classmate, friend, or family member. Ask four or five questions. For example, you can ask questions about where they live, what they do, where they are from, etc.

2. Write the interview down.

3. Exchange interviews with a partner. Is the punctuation correct?

VIDEO JOURNAL

A CONTACT JOB

A Look at the small photo. What's his job? Where is his job?

B Are there street performers in your town or city? Are they interesting?

C Watch the video and answer the questions.

1. Which city is he in?
2. Is Okotanpe a musician?
3. Where is his job?
4. Is it a difficult job?

D What is the difference between a juggler and a "contact juggler"? Where are the balls?

E Underline the correct words. Then watch the video again to check your answers.

1. There are *thirteen* / *thirty* million people in Tokyo.
2. Tokyo is a *small* / *big* city.
3. The ball is *soft* / *hard* plastic.
4. It's *boring* / *interesting* for the people in the street.
5. Okotanpe *is* / *isn't* popular.
6. Okotanpe uses *four* / *fourteen* balls.

Street performers are musicians, jugglers, and artists. This man is a juggler.

F Write five questions for Okotanpe (e.g., *Where is your job? Is it easy?*).

G Work in pairs.

Student A: Ask your questions from **F**.
Student B: You are Okotanpe. Answer the questions.

Switch roles and ask your questions.

**Contact juggler
Okotanpe**

Houses and Apartments

About 7.5 million people live in Hong Kong. Most people live in apartments.

PRONUNCIATION: Syllables and Stressed Syllables

 21 A syllable is a part of a word. Each syllable has one vowel sound. When a word has more than one syllable, we usually stress one. Listen to the syllables and the stress (underlined) in these words.

<u>house</u> (1 syllable)   <u>bed</u>room (2 syllables)   a<u>part</u>ment (3 syllables)

D **22** Listen to the word. Write the number of syllables it has and <u>underline</u> the stressed syllable.

kitchen ___2___   stairs _____   floor _____   elevator _____

yard _____   balcony _____   window _____

bathroom _____   roof _____

E **22** Listen again and repeat the words.

✓ GOAL CHECK Compare Houses

In pairs, describe and compare the houses. What is similar? What is different?

> There are two doors in this house.

GOAL Say Where Objects Are

Language Expansion: Furniture and Household Objects

A 🎧 23 Listen and repeat the words for household objects.

lamp   chair   TV   table   armchair

stove   refrigerator   bookcase   sofa   microwave   coffee table

shower   sink   bed   toilet

B Write the furniture and household objects in the correct column. You may write some objects in more than one room.

Kitchen	Dining room	Living room	Bedroom	Bathroom
stove				

C **MY WORLD** Answer the questions in pairs.

1. Which furniture and objects are in your home?

2. How many are there?

> There are two TVs. One is in the kitchen, and one is in the living room.

Grammar

Prepositions of Place

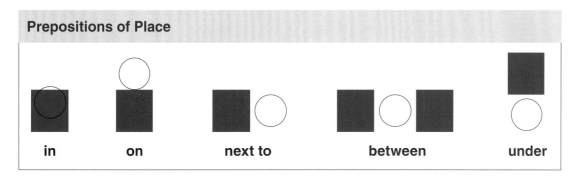

| in | on | next to | between | under |

D Complete each sentence with a preposition.

1. There's food _____ the refrigerator.

2. There's a lamp _____ the table.

3. The armchair is _____ the sofa.

4. My bedroom is _____ my parents' bedroom and my sister's bedroom.

Conversation

E ∩ 24 Listen to the conversation. Where are Tracey's keys?

Tracey: Where are my <u>keys</u>?

Kevin: Are they <u>on the table in the hall</u>?

Tracey: No, they aren't. And they aren't <u>on the kitchen table</u>.

Kevin: What about <u>in your bag</u>?

Tracey: No, they aren't there.

Kevin: Here they are! <u>On the coffee table. Next to the lamp</u>.

SPEAKING STRATEGY

Talk about Location
*Your book is **here**.* = in the same place as the speaker.
*Your keys are **there**.* = in another place.

F Practice the conversation in pairs. Switch roles and practice it again. Then change the underlined words and make a new conversation.

✓ **GOAL CHECK** Say Where Objects Are

(It's next to the sofa.)

In pairs, describe where an object is in the room. Your partner guesses the object.

Home Sweet Home?

D GOAL Give Your Opinion

Reading

A What is in the photo?

B Read about the house and complete the information.

1. Number of floors: _____
2. Rooms downstairs: _____
3. Household objects: _____
4. Number of bedrooms: _____
5. Electricity: **Yes / No**
6. Internet: **Yes / No**

C Answer the questions.

1. Is the house in Hawaii or on Mars?
2. Who lives in the house?
3. What are the scientists interested in?

D Find the matching adjectives in the article.

1. new _____*modern*_____
2. a color _____
3. not big _____
4. nice to be in _____
5. nice to look at _____

E Write the opposite adjectives from **D**.

1. big _____*small*_____
2. old _____
3. uncomfortable _____
4. ugly _____

F What do you think of the house for Mars? Is it a nice house?

 GOAL CHECK

In pairs, use adjectives to describe and give your opinion of these places.

- your house
- your office / workplace
- your classroom
- a building in your town / city

> It's a modern building.   There are offices in it.   It's ugly!

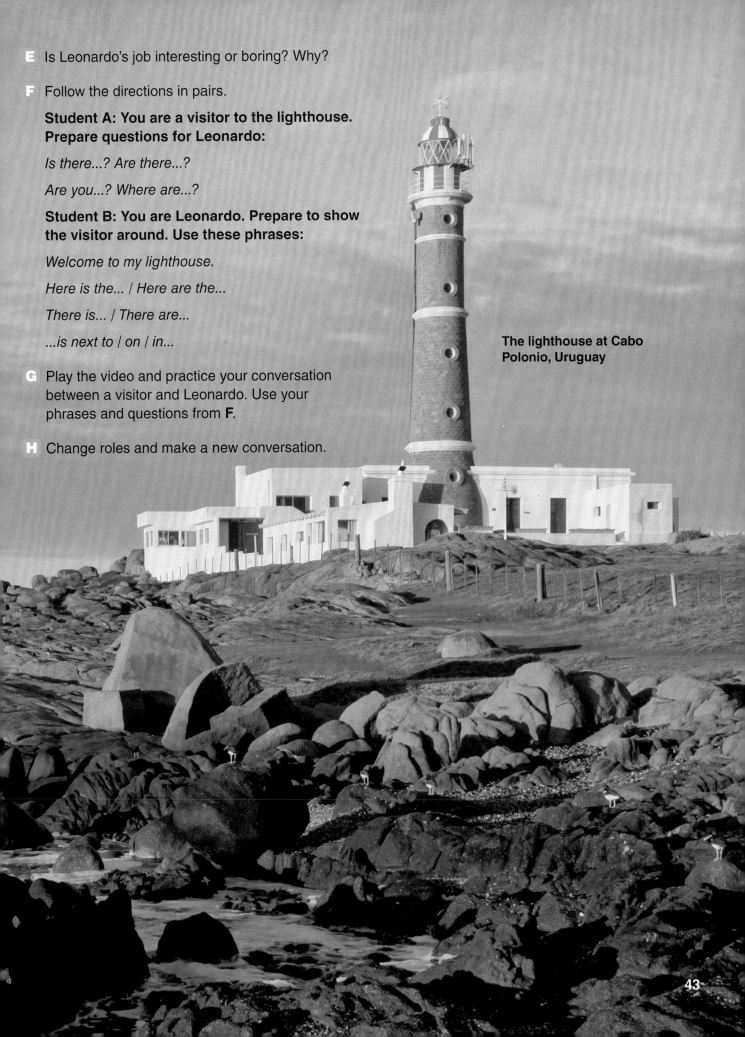

E Is Leonardo's job interesting or boring? Why?

F Follow the directions in pairs.

Student A: You are a visitor to the lighthouse. Prepare questions for Leonardo:

Is there...? Are there...?

Are you...? Where are...?

Student B: You are Leonardo. Prepare to show the visitor around. Use these phrases:

Welcome to my lighthouse.

Here is the... / Here are the...

There is... / There are...

...is next to / on / in...

The lighthouse at Cabo Polonio, Uruguay

G Play the video and practice your conversation between a visitor and Leonardo. Use your phrases and questions from **F**.

H Change roles and make a new conversation.

This man is a barber in San Cristóbal de las Casas, Chiapas, Mexico. He keeps many possessions in his shop.

Look at the photo and answer the questions.

1 Where are these people? What possessions do you see?

2 What is your favorite personal possession?

PELUQUERÍA TONO'S

TE DE PELO $50.00
O E $50.00

FERNANDO VALADES
EL DISCO DE ORO

UNIT 4 GOALS

A. Ask about Possessions

B. Present a Special Object

C. Talk about What You Have

D. Identify Similarities and Differences

E. Thank Someone for a Present

45

GOAL Ask about Possessions

Vocabulary

A Complete the names of the objects in the photos. Use the words in the box.

backpack	book	bus pass	headphones	keys	makeup
notebook	pen	phone	sunglasses	wallet	water bottle

1. b _ _ k **2.** n _ _ _ _ _ k **3.** m _ k _ u _ **4.** w _ _ _ r b _ _ tl _

5. p _ _ **6.** h _ _ dph _ _ _ s **7.** b _ _ kp _ _ _ **8.** wa _ _ _ t

9. p _ _ _ e **10.** s _ n _ l _ s _ _ s **11.** b _ s p _ _ s **12.** _ _ _ s

B Work in pairs. Close your books. Remember and say the objects in **A**.

C Take turns. Say the objects in the pictures. Which objects are in both pictures?

Student A

Student B

There's a bus pass in this bag.

There isn't a bus pass in this bag. There are notebooks in both bags!

Grammar

Demonstratives

	Singular	Plural
Near ←	**This** is your bag. Is **this** your bag?	**These** are not my books. Are **these** your books?
Far →	**That** is your bag. Is **that** your bag?	**Those** are not my pens. Are **those** your pens?

D Match the questions and answers. There can be more than one correct answer.

Question

1. Is this your pen? _____
2. Are those your keys? _____
3. Are these your glasses? _____
4. Is that your dictionary? _____

Answer

a. Yes, they are.
b. No, it isn't.
c. Yes, it is.
d. No, they aren't.

E Complete the questions and answers.

1. (far) ___Are those___ your glasses?   No, ___they aren't___.
2. (far) _____ your book?   Yes, _____.
3. (near) _____ your wallet?   No, _____.
4. (near) _____ your keys?   No, _____.
5. (far) _____ your bags?   Yes, _____.

F **MY WORLD** Work in pairs. Tell your partner what is in your bag. Use demonstratives.

✓ GOAL CHECK Ask about Possessions

Play a game in small groups. Each student puts four objects from their bag in the middle of the table.

1. Student 1 asks Student 2 about one object.

Is this your pen?   Yes, it is.   No, it isn't.

Are those your keys?   Yes, they are.   No, they aren't.

2. A *yes* answer is 1 point. A *no* answer is 0 points.
3. Next, Student 2 asks Student 3 about an object, and so on.
4. At the end, who has the most points?

GOAL Present a Special Object

**Hetain Patel is an artist.
This is one of his artworks.**

Listening

A In pairs, look at the photo of Hetain Patel. What is the object?

B 🎧 26 Listen to a podcast about Hetain. Is your answer in **A** correct?

C 🎧 26 Listen again. Circle **T** for *true* or **F** for *false*.

1. Hetain Patel is from England.	**T**	**F**
2. Jerome's job is very boring.	**T**	**F**
3. It's Hetain's father's car.	**T**	**F**
4. The car has hands and feet.	**T**	**F**
5. The car is similar to a Transformer robot.	**T**	**F**
6. Their online video is very popular.	**T**	**F**

Grammar

Possession							
Subject Pronoun	I	you	he	she	it	we	they
Possessive Adjective	my	your	his	her	its	our	their

Singular Nouns	Plural Nouns
Hetain's car	the couple's cars
the student's house (one student)	the students' house (more than one student)

Grandparents give a present to their grandson in Kuala Lumpur, Malaysia, to celebrate Eid al-Fitr, a religious holiday.

Communication

A Look at the photo. Why does this person have a present? What special day is it?

B In your country, what are presents for?

- birthdays?
- weddings?
- a new baby?
- the New Year?
- religious days?
- other days?

C In groups, discuss what presents are good for each person and situation.

1. It's your brother's wedding.
2. Your sister has a new baby.
3. It's your teacher's birthday.
4. Your friend has a New Year's party.
5. Your grandparents have their 50th wedding anniversary.

> A book is a good present for my friend.

> I think a book is boring. What about a new bag?

Writing

D Read the emails and messages. Which person in **C** is each from?

1.

Hi,

How's it going?

Thanks for the new lamp. It's great in our new house.
Come over and see it soon!

All the best,
Peter (and Tracey!)

2.

Hello everyone!
Thanks very much for the chocolates. They're delicious!
See you next week (and your test on Monday is canceled ☺).

3.

Dear Martin,

Thank you so much for the flowers. They are on our kitchen table, and they are beautiful. What a wonderful grandson!

Love,
Grandma

E Complete the table below with phrases from **D**.

WRITING SKILL: Short Emails and Messages
Start: Hi, _____, _____
Thanks: _____, _____, _____ *Thank you so much* _____
Finish: _____, _____ *See you next week* _____, _____

✓ **GOAL CHECK** Thank Someone for a Present

1. It's your birthday, and you have a present from a friend. It's a book. Write a short email to your friend to say thank you. Use some of the phrases above.

2. Exchange your email with a partner. Which phrases are in the email?

VIDEO JOURNAL

TYLER BIKES ACROSS AMERICA

A Read about Tyler Metcalfe and look at the map. Where is his trip?

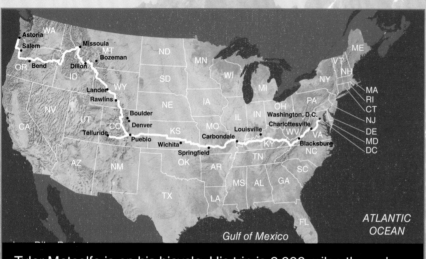

Tyler Metcalfe is on his bicycle. His trip is 6,000 miles through 11 states across the US.

B What possessions do you think Tyler has on his trip (e.g., a bike, a helmet)?

C Watch the first part of the video. Check (✓) what Tyler has with him.

- ✓ a bicycle
- ✓ a helmet
- ☐ bicycle bags
- ☐ a wallet
- ☐ a sleeping bag
- ☐ blankets
- ☐ a tent
- ☐ gloves

- ☐ keys
- ☐ a hat
- ☐ a raincoat
- ☐ a camping stove
- ☐ lots of food
- ☐ a camera
- ☐ books
- ☐ a map

Tyler Metcalfe rides his bike in Grand Teton National Park, Wyoming, US.

D Watch the first part of the video again. Why does Tyler have ...

1. a tent? _Sometimes there aren't hotels._

2. a raincoat? _____

3. a camping stove _____

4. a camera? _____

E Look at Tyler's route on the map and watch the second part of the video.

F Watch the video again. Match 1–6 to the state.

1. a horse _c_
2. a hill ____
3. a train ____
4. Yellowstone National Park ____
5. a hotel ____
6. a ship and the ocean ____

a. Wyoming
b. Missouri
c. Virginia
d. Montana
e. Kentucky
f. Washington

G In groups, plan a seven-day trip through your country, or to different countries.

1. List the place or places to go to each day.

2. List the possessions you have for the trip.

3. Join another group. Present your trip and the possessions you have.

Daily Activities

A train goes by in Shinjuku, Japan, home of the busiest train station in the world.

E MY WORLD Do you commute to work or school? How long is your commute? How many miles is it? Tell the class. Who has the longest commute?

PRONUNCIATION: Falling Intonation on Statements and Information Questions

At the end of most statements and information questions, a person's intonation falls slightly. The speaker's voice starts high and falls toward the end of the sentence.

F 🎧 33 Listen and repeat.

1. **A:** What time do you get up?

   B: I get up at six o'clock.

2. **A:** What time do they have lunch?

   B: They have lunch at one thirty.

3. **A:** What time does David go to bed?

   B: He goes to bed at eleven o'clock.

G Take turns reading the questions and answers in pairs. Use falling intonation.

1. **A:** What time does Salma start work? **B:** She starts work at eight thirty.

2. **A:** What time do they get up? **B:** They get up at a quarter to seven.

3. **A:** What time do you finish work? **B:** I finish work at six o'clock.

Communication

H Write two more questions in the table. Then interview two classmates.

What time do you...?	Classmate 1	Classmate 2
1. leave home?		
2. get to work / school?		
3. have lunch?		
4.		
5.		

✓ **GOAL CHECK** Compare People's Daily Routines

In pairs, describe and compare your classmates' daily routines. Use the information in **H**. How similar are they?

> Alice and Ricardo leave home at 8 o'clock.

> Jorge gets to work at eight thirty and Saki gets to school at eight forty-five.

GOAL Talk about Activities at Work and School

Language Expansion: Work and School Activities

A Match the verbs to the photos.

| ~~check~~ | go | meet | take | talk | text | travel | write |

1. __check__ email

2. _____ to class

3. _____ to people on the phone

4. _____ to other countries

5. _____ reports

6. _____ a test

7. _____ friends

8. _____ clients

B Write the activities in **A** in the table for you.

Activities I do every day	Activities I do every week	Activities I do every few months	Activities I never do

C Write five more activities you do at work or school. Discuss in pairs.

Grammar

Simple Present Questions and Answers	
Question	Short Answer
Do I / you / we / they **meet** clients every day?	Yes, I / you / we / they **do**. No, I / you / we / they **don't**.
Does he / she **meet** clients every day?	Yes, he / she **does**. No, he / she **doesn't**.

Adverbs of Frequency		
I **always** check my email.		100%
I **sometimes** meet clients.	50%	
I **never** write reports.	0%	

D Write the correct form of *do* in these questions and answers.

1. **A:** _____ you meet clients every day? **B:** No, I _____. I never meet clients.

2. **A:** _____ Ali write reports every day? **B:** Yes, he _____.

3. **A:** _____ Chris and Diana travel a lot? **B:** Yes, they _____.

4. **A:** _____ Rina go to the gym every day? **B:** No, she _____. She goes every week.

5. **A:** _____ you check emails every morning? **B:** Yes, we _____.

E Write about your work or school. Complete the sentences using *always*, *sometimes*, or *never*.

1. I _____ wake up at seven o'clock.

2. I _____ text friends at work or school.

3. I _____ take tests.

4. I _____ go to the gym.

5. I _____ write reports.

Conversation

F 🎧 34 Listen to the conversation. What does Brenda do in the morning and in the afternoon? Does she always travel?

Yoshi: What's your job?

Brenda: I'm a personal assistant at a travel agency.

Yoshi: What do you do at work?

Brenda: Oh, in the morning I check emails, and in the afternoon, I go to meetings. It isn't very interesting.

Yoshi: Do you travel?

Brenda: I sometimes meet clients in places like Rio and Singapore.

Yoshi: Not interesting? It sounds fantastic to me!

SPEAKING STRATEGY

Asking Questions
Are you...?
What's your...?
Do you...?
What do you...?

REAL LANGUAGE

Use *like* to give examples.

G Practice the conversation in pairs. Switch roles and practice again.

✓ GOAL CHECK Talk about Activities at Work and School

1. Write questions to ask a partner. Find out what he or she does at work or school:
   - in the morning.
   - in the afternoon.
   - always, sometimes, or never.

2. Ask and answer the questions with your partner.

What do you do?   Do you...?

I'm a student.   In the morning, I...   I sometimes write...

D GOAL Present a Report

Reading

A In groups, list all of the objects with screens in your daily lives (e.g., TVs, phones, laptops, etc).

B Read the first paragraph of the article. Underline the objects and activities with screens.

C Read the rest of the article. Write the correct numbers in the table.

1. Hours we sleep every day		hours
2. Hours we work and commute		hours
3. Hours for survival activities		hours
4. Percentage of personal time with screens in 2007		%
5. Percentage of personal time with screens in 2015		%
6. Percentage of personal time with screens in 2017		%

D **MY WORLD** Look at the last paragraph. Adam Alter thinks we need more personal time without screens. Do you agree? Why?

E Do a class survey. Interview three people in your class with these questions and write down their answers.

1. How many hours do you sleep?
2. How many hours do you work or study and commute?
3. How many hours do you have for survival time?
4. How many hours do you have for personal time?
5. What percentage of your personal time is with a screen?

F Make a table or chart about the answers to your survey in **E**. Use the table in **C** or the bar chart in the article as a model.

GOAL CHECK

Present your table or chart to a partner. Are your results similar? Are they similar to Adam Alter's report?

We spend more and more of our daily lives with screens: TVs, laptops, smartphones, tablets, video games, smartwatches. Of course, screens are important in our lives. We check the time on them in the morning, we send emails with them at work, and we watch TV or play games with them at night. But are we too connected?

This chart from Adam Alter, a professor at New York University, shows how we spend our time, and how much time we spend on screens. It shows three different years: 2007, 2015, and 2017. Some activities don't change. Every year, humans sleep for about eight hours per day. We work and commute for about eight or nine hours a day. Then, for three hours a day, we do "survival" activities: we eat, we take a shower, we take care of children.

Finally, the chart shows four to five hours for "personal" time, or free time. In this time, we go to the gym, we play games, we have hobbies, we meet friends. It's very important time! But over time, we spend more and more of this personal time on screens. In the chart, red shows our personal time with screens. In 2007, 50% of our personal time is with screens. In 2015, it's about 70%. In 2017, it's about 90%!

Overall, Adam Alter thinks this change is bad. He thinks we need more personal time without screens, and more personal time for sports, hobbies, and friends. But do people want to change the amount of time they look at screens?

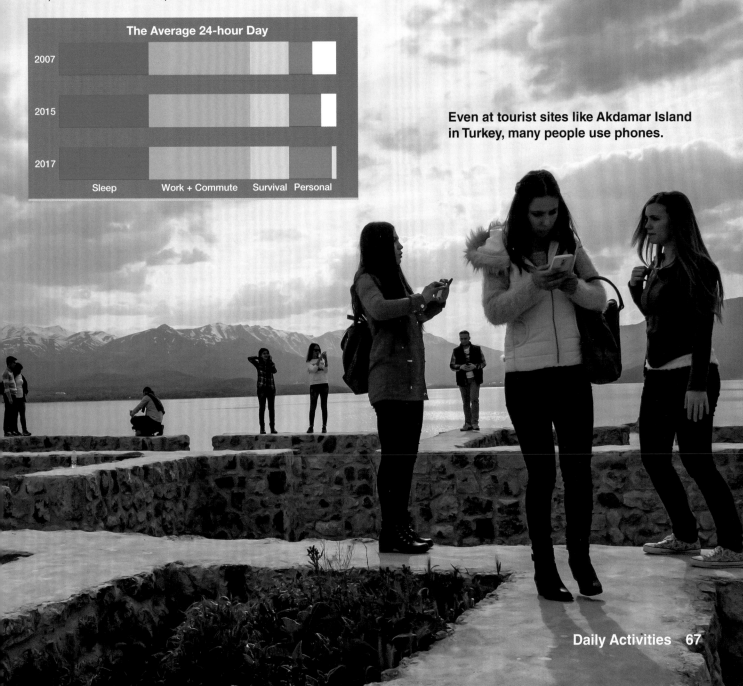

The Average 24-hour Day

2007				
2015				
2017				
Sleep		Work + Commute	Survival	Personal

Even at tourist sites like Akdamar Island in Turkey, many people use phones.

A study at Baylor University in the US says that writing to-do lists helps people sleep better at night.

Writing

A Do you write to-do lists? Why do people write them?

GRAMMAR: Imperatives	
Affirmative	Negative
Check my email. **Answer** the questions.	**Don't be** late for your lesson. **Don't use** your phone in class.

B Complete the texts. Write the imperative verbs.

> don't do   don't stay up   finish   go   meet   wait

A.

TO DO:
- Check my emails
- (1) _____ to 11:00 meeting
- Have lunch at 1:00 with Peter
- (2) _____ my report

B.

Good luck with your test tomorrow, everyone. Tonight:

1. Relax! (3) _____ any more work.
2. Go to bed early! (4) _____ late.
3. Sleep for 8 hours!

All the best, Your teacher

C.

> Hi,
>
> (5) _____ me tomorrow. Take the train to Central Station. If I'm late, (6) _____ in the cafe at the station. See you at noon.

C Which text (A, B, or C) is...

1. instructions to a friend? _____

2. advice to some students? _____

3. to the writer (not another person)? _____

WRITING SKILL: Lists and Notes
We often use the imperative form with lists, notes, and short messages. When you write lists and notes, use bullet points or numbers.

D Think about tomorrow and write a to-do list for yourself. Then exchange your lists in pairs. What imperative forms does your partner use?

Communication

E In the article in Lesson D, Adam Alter is worried because people spend a lot of their personal time with screens. Read the Do / Don't lists below. Do you agree with them? Why?

<u>HOW TO HAVE PERSONAL TIME WITHOUT SCREENS</u>

DO!	**DON'T!**
• Turn off your phone at dinner.	• Don't watch TV all night.
• Talk to your family and friends.	• Don't play computer games for more than two hours a day.
• Get some exercise. Go to the gym.	• Don't check work emails at home.

F Choose a topic in groups. Discuss and write Do / Don't lists using the imperative form.

- How to have fun on weekends
- How to learn another language
- How to get more exercise

✓ **GOAL CHECK** Give Advice and Instructions

Work with another group and present your Do / Don't list from **F**. Give them your advice and instructions.

VIDEO JOURNAL

AROUND THE WORLD IN 24 HOURS

A Read about the times in five cities. Write the correct time for each city.

> It's noon in London. Moscow is two hours ahead of London. Mexico City is eight hours behind Moscow. Tokyo is fourteen hours ahead of Mexico City, and New Delhi is three and a half hours behind Tokyo.

Mexico City	London	Moscow	New Delhi	Tokyo

B Find out the answers in pairs.

1. What time is it now in your country?
2. What time is it now in the cities in **A**?
3. How many hours are you ahead of, or behind, the cities?

C Watch the video. What time is it in each place?

1. Hawaii 5 am
2. Paris
3. San Francisco
4. Melbourne
5. Namibia
6. Portland

7. Croatia
8. Kerala
9. Monaco
10. Norway
11. Bogota

D Watch the video again and answer the questions.

1. On what days is the food market open in Paris?
2. What does Melbourne have lots of?
3. What is hot in Namibia?
4. Which meal do you eat in Portland?
5. Who goes home at 6 pm?
6. What two things do people spend in Monaco?
7. Is it dark at night in Norway?
8. In Bogota, where do people go in the middle of the night?

The northern lights at midnight over Olstind Mountain, Lofoten Islands, Norway

E In groups, plan a similar video about your town, city, or country. Choose five times of day and five photographs of places and activities to show. Write your ideas in the table.

Time of Day	Place and Activity

F Work with another group. Present your ideas for the video.

Central Station in Rio De Janeiro, Brazil, is home to the SuperVia train company. SuperVia carries 750 million passengers a year!

NAO EMBARQUE →

UNIT 6 GOALS

A. Ask For and Give Directions

B. Create a Tour

C. Compare Types of Transportation

D. Plan a Bicycle Day

E. Give Advice to Travelers

Vocabulary

A Look at the places on the map. Match the activities to the place.

1. Buy food for the week _____

2. Ask for information about the town _____

3. Eat a meal (3 places) _____

4. Look at old objects _____

5. Read a book _____

6. Stay the night (2 places) _____

7. Watch a movie _____

8. Send mail _____

9. Get some money _____

10. Go shopping for clothes _____

11. Relax outside _____

12. Go dancing _____

13. Take transportation (2 places) _____

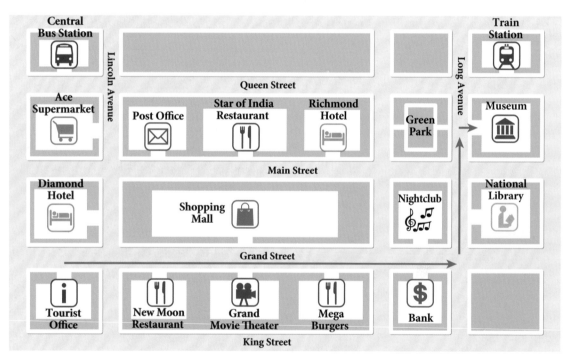

B **MY WORLD** Which places do you often go to in your town or city? What do you do there? Tell your partner.

> I go to the movie theater a lot, because I like watching movies.

> I go to the shopping mall on weekends. I like shopping for clothes!

C 🎧 36 Read and listen to this conversation at a tourist information office. Follow the red arrow on the map in **A** for the directions.

Tourist: Is the museum near here?

Receptionist: Yes, it's on Long Avenue.

Tourist: How do I get there?

Receptionist: Go out of this building and turn right. Go across Lincoln Avenue and walk straight down Grand Street to the library. It's on the corner of Grand Street and Long Avenue. Turn left and walk a block to Main Street. The museum is on the next block, on the right.

Tourist: Thank you very much!

Receptionist: You're welcome.

Grammar

Prepositions of Place

Richmond hotel is **on** the corner of the street. The museum is **across from** the library. Star of India restaurant is **between** the post office and Richmond Hotel. Richmond Hotel is **at** 225 Main Street. Green Park is **near** the train station and the museum.	*Prepositions of place are often after the verb *to be*.

Prepositions of Movement

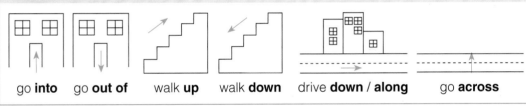

go **into**   go **out of**   walk **up**   walk **down**   drive **down / along**   go **across**

*Prepositions of movement are after verbs of movement (e.g., *walk, go, drive, move, run*)

D Read the conversation in **C** again. Underline the prepositions of place and movement.

E Complete the directions with the prepositions.

Tourist: Is the movie theater (1) _____ here?

Local: Yes, it's (2) _____ Grand Street. From the train station, go right on Queen Street and then turn left onto Long Avenue. Walk (3) _____ Long Avenue for two blocks. Go (4) _____ Grand Street to the bank. It's (5) _____ the corner. Turn right and walk one block. The movie theater is on the next block (6) _____ Mega Burgers and New Moon Restaurant.

across
between
down
near
on
on

✓ GOAL CHECK Ask For and Give Directions

In pairs, take turns asking for and giving directions.

Student A: Start at the train station. Ask for directions to three places.

Student B: Start at the bus station. Ask for directions to three different places.

The historic center of Paraty, Brazil

Listening

A 🎧 37 A tour guide is with a group of tourists in Matriz Square in Paraty, Brazil. Listen to different parts of the walking tour. What places on the map do they go to?

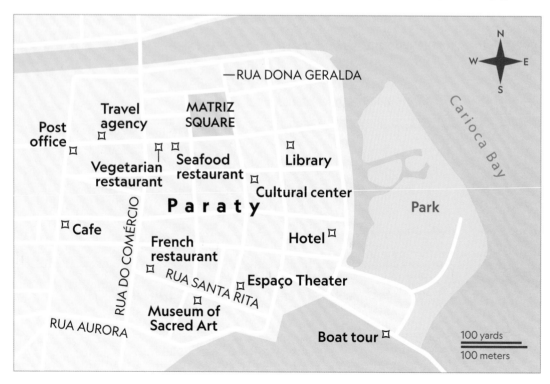

B 🎧 37 Read the sentences about the tour and underline the correct words. Then listen again and check.

1. Amanda is *the tour guide* / *a tourist*.

2. Paraty is *an old* / *a modern* city.

3. *There are* / *There aren't* cars or buses in the center.

4. The theater is on the *left* / *right*.

5. The art museum is *small* / *famous*.

6. A tourist wants to send a *letter* / *postcard*.

7. *They go to* / *They don't go to* the post office.

PRONUNCIATION: *Yes* / *No* Questions and Short Answers

In *Yes* / *No* questions, a speaker's intonation usually rises at the end of the question. In short answers, the intonation usually falls on *Yes* or *No* and then falls again at the end of the answer.

C 🎧 38 Listen and repeat.

1. **A:** Is there a post office near here? **B:** Yes, there is.

2. **A:** Is the bus station on Main Street? **B:** No, it isn't.

3. **A:** Is the museum on this square? **B:** Yes, it is.

D In pairs, take turns reading the questions and answers.

1. **A:** Is there a hotel near here? **B:** No, there isn't.

2. **A:** Is the library next to the museum? **B:** Yes, it is.

3. **A:** Is there a tourist office in this town? **B:** No, there isn't.

Communication

E In pairs, answer these questions about your town or city and take notes.

1. Is there a museum? What is it called? Where is it?

2. Is there a park? Where is it?

3. Are there good restaurants? Where are they?

4. What other interesting places for tourists are in your town or city?

✓ **GOAL CHECK** Create a Tour

In pairs, create a two-hour tour of your town or city.

1. Choose the places on the tour.

2. Draw a map and put the places on it.

3. Prepare notes about the places (e.g., old? modern? interesting? famous?).

4. Work with another pair and give your tour with the map.

GOAL Compare Types of Transportation

Language Expansion: Ground Transportation

A Read the website and answer the questions.

1. Where do the types of transportation leave from?

2. Where does the bus go to?

3. How long does a taxi take?

4. How much does the subway cost?

5. What do you need to rent a car?

REAL LANGUAGE

$4 = *four dollars*
$4.50 = *four dollars and fifty cents*

Airport Transportation
After your airplane lands at the airport, there are many ways to get downtown.

Subway
Take the subway. $2.50

Bus
Take the A100 bus to Central Station. $4.50

Taxi
Take a taxi (about 30 minutes).
Approximately $50

Car
Rent a car. You have to have a passport and driver's license. $120 a day

Train
Take a train. You have to change trains at Midway Station. $10

B In pairs, complete the chart with the costs and types of transportation.

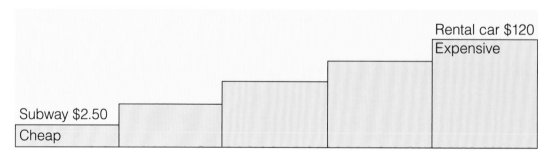

Rental car $120
Expensive

Subway $2.50
Cheap

Grammar

C Compare the sentences. Then write the correct number.

1. You have to have your passport.

2. You have your passport.

Which sentence means:

a. Your passport is with you now. _____

b. You need your passport with you at the airport. It's required! _____

78 Unit 6

Have to		
Statement	Question	Short Answer
I / You / We / They **have to** take a taxi.	**Do** I / you / we / they **have to** change trains?	Yes, I / you / we / they **do**. No, I / you / we / they **don't**.
He / She **has to** change buses.	**Does** he / she **have to** take a taxi?	Yes, he / she **does**. No, he / she **doesn't**.
Have to is used to show obligation.		

D Complete the sentences with the correct form of *have to* or *do*.

1. **A:** Do we _____ take a bus?   **B:** No, we _____ take a train.

2. **A:** _____ I have to change trains?   **B:** Yes, you _____.

3. **A:** _____ Susana have to take the subway?   **B:** No, she _____ rent a car.

4. **A:** _____ he have to go to the meeting?   **B:** No, he _____.

Conversation

E 🎧 39 Listen to the conversation. Where does the tourist have to go? How long does it take?

Tourist: Excuse me, how do I get to <u>the airport</u>?

Assistant: Take <u>the subway</u>. You have to <u>change trains</u>, but it's cheap.

Tourist: How long does it take?

Assistant: <u>About an hour</u>.

Tourist: Oh! But I have to get there by <u>two thirty</u>. And I have four bags!

Assistant: Two thirty! <u>In half an hour</u>? OK, you have to take <u>a taxi</u> then. It's expensive, but it's fast.

SPEAKING STRATEGY

Talking about Times and Costs
How much is it?
  Four dollars.
  It's cheap / expensive.
How long does it take?
  An hour.
  It's slow / fast.

F Practice the conversation in pairs. Switch roles and practice it again. Then change the underlined words and make a new conversation.

 GOAL CHECK Compare Types of Transportation

1. You work at a new airport. Complete the *You* column with new times and prices from the airport to downtown (e.g., *bus = 1 hour / $5.50*).

	You	**Your Partner**
Bus		
Taxi		
Subway		
Train		

2. In pairs, ask about your partner's times and prices. Write the answers in the table.

3. Compare your answers. Is your transportation fast or slow? Cheap or expensive?

GOAL Plan a Bicycle Day

Reading

A Look at the photo and the title of the article. What day is it? Where are the cars?

B Read the article and write the paragraph number (1–3).

a. Paragraph _____ is about how local people have fun at Ciclovía.

b. Paragraph _____ is about transportation in Bogotá.

c. Paragraph _____ is about why Ciclovía is popular.

C Look at the groups of words from the article. Delete one word that doesn't belong in each group.

Countries: Colombia, ~~Europe~~, China, New Zealand
Motor vehicles: bicycles, cars, taxis, motorcycles
Vehicles without motors: bicycles, wheelchairs, buses, skateboards
Jobs: fitness instructor, manager, musician, salsa
Groups of people: citizens, streets, human beings, Bogotanos

D Read the article again and answer the questions.

1. What do these numbers refer to in paragraph 1?

   75   9,000   50,000   500,000   1,600,000

2. What can you do at a "Fun Stop"?

3. Why does Bibiana Sarmiento think Ciclovía is a good idea? Do you agree with her?

✓ GOAL CHECK

1. Work in pairs. You have to start a Bicycle Way for your town or city. Discuss and decide:

   • What day (or days) is your Bicycle Way?

   • How often is it? (e.g., every week? every month?)

   • How many miles do you close to motor vehicles?

   • How many "Fun Stops" are there? What do people do at them?

2. Join another group. Present your plans.

> Our Bicycle Way is on ...

> We close 50 miles ...

D Watch the second part of the video. Number the actions in the order you see them.

___1___ Princess Leia waits for the subway train.

_____ The stormtroopers take Princess Leia to the doors.

_____ She reads a book.

_____ Darth Vader gets on the train.

_____ The stormtroopers and Princess Leia get off the train.

_____ Princess Leia and Darth Vader talk to each other.

_____ Stormtroopers get on the train.

E Improv Everywhere wants to make people laugh. Do people laugh in the video? What makes you laugh?

F In groups, plan another performance for Improv Everywhere.

1. Where do you want to do the performance? On a train? A bus? In the street? A park?

2. Which movie do you want to perform?

3. How many actors do you need? Do they need costumes?

G Present your ideas from **F** to the class.

It's the weekend, and this family in Iraq is having a picnic at Lake Dukan north of the city of Slemani.

E 🎧 44 Listen to the expressions. Notice how some words sound connected.

1. Hello, this_is Mandy.

2. Can_I call you back?

3. Can you speak_up?

4. What_are you doing?

5. I'm in_a meeting.

F 🎧 44 Close your books and listen to the sentences again. How many words do you hear in each sentence? Write them down. (e.g., *What are you doing? = 4 words*.)

Communication

G Look at the chart. Think about where you are and what you are doing at these times. Fill in your information.

Day	Time	Location	Activity
Friday	8:00 a.m.		
	1:00 p.m.		
	10:00 p.m.		
Saturday	7:00 a.m.		
	3:00 p.m.		
	8:00 p.m.		

✓ GOAL CHECK Make a Phone Call

Choose a day and time from the chart. Role-play a phone call with your partner. Find out their location and activity.

Hello, who's calling?

Where are you? · I'm on the train.

What are you doing? · I'm going to school.

Sorry, can you speak up? · Can I call you back?

GOAL Talk about Abilities

Language Expansion: Sports

A Match the sports to the correct photos.

play basketball	play soccer	play tennis	ride a bike
run	skateboard	ski	swim

1. _____ 2. _____ 3. _____ 4. _____

5. _____ 6. _____ 7. _____ 8. _____

REAL LANGUAGE

We use **play** for competitive sports with a ball: *play tennis / soccer / basketball*
We use **go** for sports with *-ing*: *go swimming / running / skiing*

B Answer the questions. Then interview two classmates.

Do you ever...	Me	Classmate 1	Classmate 2
play soccer?			
go skiing?			
go swimming?			
go running?			
play basketball?			
go skateboarding?			
play tennis?			
go biking?			

Do you ever play soccer?   Yes, sometimes.   No, never.

Grammar

Can for Ability			
Statement	Negative	*Yes / No* Question	Short Answer
I / You / She / He / We / They **can** swim.	He **cannot** swim. She **can't** play guitar.	**Can** you ski?	Yes, I **can**. No, I **can't**.

C Write about yourself. Complete the sentences with *can* or *can't*.

1. I _____ swim.
2. I _____ play soccer.
3. I _____ play golf.
4. I _____ ski.
5. I _____ play tennis.

D Complete the conversations.

1. **A:** _____ play volleyball?

   B: No, I can't, but I _____ play soccer.

2. **A:** _____ Damien swim?

   B: Yes, _____.

Conversation

E 🎧 45 Listen to the conversation. What can each classmate do?

Julie: Hi, Yumi. This is Rosa. It's her first day, but she can speak English <u>very well</u>.

Yumi: Hi, Rosa! Welcome.

Rosa: Hi, Yumi. How's it going?

Julie: So, you both play musical instruments. Rosa can <u>play the guitar</u>.

Rosa: Well, I'm learning.

Yumi: Great! I can play <u>the piano</u>.

Rosa: How well can you play?

Julie: She can play <u>very well</u>.

Rosa: What about you, Julie? Can you play a musical instrument?

Julie: No, I can't.

Yumi: But Julie is great at sports. She can <u>ski</u> really well, and she's on the soccer team!

F In groups of three, practice the conversation in **E**. Switch roles and practice it again.

G Change the underlined words and make a new conversation.

✔ GOAL CHECK Talk about Abilities

1. Prepare three *Can you ... ?* questions about different abilities (e.g., sports, musical instruments, languages, etc.).

2. Interview a partner with your three questions. Find out how well they can do something.

> Can you speak Chinese?

> Yes, very well.

> How well can you play basketball?

3. Join another pair. Tell them about your partner's abilities.

> Jose can speak Spanish and English very well.

> He can't play a musical instrument, but he can sing!

D GOAL Explain How to Play Something

Reading

A Look at the photo and read the first paragraph of the article. What are hybrid sports?

B Read the article. Circle T for *true* or F for *false*.

1. Football tennis is popular in two countries.   T   F
2. You can use your hands in football tennis.   T   F
3. You can watch chess boxing in different countries.   T   F
4. In chess boxing, you play chess for 11 rounds.   T   F
5. You have to cycle and juggle in joggling.   T   F
6. At the World Joggling Championships, there are different races.   T   F

C Match these words from the article to the definitions.

1. competition __c__
2. race _____
3. team _____
4. player _____
5. net _____
6. strong _____

a. a person who plays sports
b. opposite of *weak*
c. an activity between people with a winner
d. a competition between runners over a distance
e. the thing between players in tennis
f. a group of players

D Answer these questions in groups.

1. What is the most popular sport in your country?
2. Do you have a favorite athlete or team?
3. Do you ever play sports in competitions?

E Read the rules for football tennis. Underline the verb forms.

You need two teams (of two players).
You can't use your hands.

Then underline the rules for chess boxing and joggling in the article.

✓ GOAL CHECK

1. In pairs, choose a sport or game and write two or three rules for it.
2. Join another pair and read your rules. Can you guess the sport or game?

D Answer the questions about Danny. Then watch the video to check your answers.

1. Where does Danny come from?

2. Where does Danny ride his bike?

3. Do people think Danny is good?

4. What is Danny's challenge?

5. What is easy about riding over the bridge? What is difficult?

6. What is Danny looking for now?

E In pairs, watch the video with NO sound and describe what Danny is doing (e.g., *He's riding on a wall, he's riding on one wheel*, etc.).

F Match each person with a challenge.

1. soccer player
_____

2. student _____

3. skier _____

4. musician _____

5. teacher _____

a. get better grades

b. go faster

c. learn to play something new

d. score more goals

e. help students pass the test

G Write down two personal challenges. Then work in groups and ask each other about your personal challenges.

Clothes

The men in this dance group from Johannesburg, South Africa, all wear the same clothes.

UNIT 8 GOALS

A. Ask about Clothes

B. Buy Clothes

C. Express Likes and Dislikes

D. Talk about Personal Qualities

E. Describe Your Favorites

101

GOAL Ask about Clothes

Vocabulary

A 🎧 47 Match the words to the photos. Then listen and repeat the words.

coat	dress
hat	jacket
jeans	pants
scarf	shirt
shoes	skirt
socks	sweater
tie	T-shirt

1. _____

2. _____

3. _____

4. _____

5. _____

6. _____

7. _____

8. _____

9. _____

10. _____

11. _____

12. _____

13. _____

14. _____

WORD FOCUS

Wear is the verb you use with clothes.

B In pairs, ask and answer the questions.

1. What clothes do you normally wear to work or school? on weekends?

2. What clothes do you never wear?

C Look at the pictures. Complete the sentences. Notice the words in blue.

1. Ruben is trying on _____.

2. Lucy is paying for the _____ by credit card.

3. The sales assistant is showing her a _____.

Grammar

<table>
<tr><th colspan="3">Can / Could for Polite Requests</th></tr>
<tr><th>Requests</th><th>Affirmative Response</th><th>Negative Response</th></tr>
<tr>
<td>Can I try on these shoes?
Can I pay with cash?
Could you show me
another shirt, please?
Could you repeat that?</td>
<td>Of course.
Yes, sure.</td>
<td>I'm sorry, but… (give reason)
I'm afraid (that)… (give reason)</td>
</tr>
<tr><td colspan="3">*Could is more polite than can.</td></tr>
</table>

D You are a clothing store customer. Write polite requests for the sales assistant.

1. You want to see some shoes. <u>Could you show me some shoes, please?</u>

2. You see a sweater and want to try it on. _____

3. You want to pay by credit card. _____

4. You want to see some pants. _____

Conversation

E 🎧 48 Write the missing words in the conversation. Then listen and check.

Zoe: I like your dress. I don't have anything nice to wear to the party …

Jill: Maybe you can wear my other dress.

Zoe: That'd be great. (1) _____ I see it, please?

Jill: Sure. Here you are.

Zoe: Thanks! (2) _____ I try it on?

Jill: Yes, of (3) _____.

Zoe: Sorry, but it doesn't fit. Can I try on a different dress?

Jill: I'm (4) _____ that I only have two nice dresses and I'm wearing the other one.

F Practice two similar conversations in pairs, starting with these phrases.

Conversation 1: "I'm cold. I don't have anything warm to wear."

Conversation 2: "The airline lost my suitcase. I don't have any extra clothes."

✔ **GOAL CHECK** Ask about Clothes

Role-play this conversation in pairs. Then switch roles and repeat the conversation.

Student A: You have a job interview, but you don't have any nice clothes. Ask Student B for help with some clothes.

Student B: Your friend has a problem. Offer some of your clothes.

GOAL Buy Clothes

Vocabulary

A Look at the photo. Point at and say the colors. Which of the two colors are not in the photo?

black	brown	dark blue	dark green	light blue	light green
orange	pink	purple	red	white	yellow

B **MY WORLD** What color are your clothes today? What is your favorite color for clothes? Where do you normally buy your clothes?

Listening

C 🎧 49 Listen to four conversations in a clothing store. Write the answers to the questions in the table.

Conversation	What color?	What clothing?
1	dark blue	tie
2		
3		
4		

D 🎧 49 In one conversation, the customer does not buy anything. Which conversation? Why doesn't the customer buy anything? Listen to check your answers.

E Who says these sentences? The sales assistant (S) or the customer (C)?

1. Can I help you? ____
2. I'm looking for a tie. ____
3. Do you have any? ____
4. I'll take it. ____
5. Do you want to pay by cash or credit card? ____
6. Could I see some shoes, please? ____
7. Do you have anything in light brown? ____

8. How much are they? ____
9. Can I try on one of those blue jackets? ____
10. What size are you? ____
11. I'm sorry, we don't have any. ____
12. OK, thanks anyway. ____
13. I'd like to look at the shirts. ____
14. The shirts are $12 each. ____

F 🎧 49 Listen again and check your answers in **D**.

PRONUNCIATION: *Could you*

We pronounce the full form of *could you* as "kud yu" – /kʊd ju/. The reduced form is "kudyuh" or "kudjuh" – /kʊdjə/ or /kʊdʒə/. We use the full form in formal speech. The reduced form is more informal.

G 🎧 50 Listen and check (✓) the box of the form you hear. Then take turns reading the sentences using the reduced forms.

	Full Form	Reduced Form
1. Could you help me, please?	✓	
2. Could you help me, please?		✓
3. Could you bring a large jacket?		
4. Could you bring a large jacket?		
5. Could you repeat that?		
6. Could you repeat that?		

Communication

H Complete the shopping list.

My shopping list			
Clothes I would like to buy	shoes		
Color	red		
Size	8		
Maximum price	$50		

✓ GOAL CHECK Buy Clothes

In pairs, role-play buying the clothes in **H**. First, Student A is the customer and Student B is the sales assistant. Then switch roles.

C GOAL Express Likes and Dislikes

Language Expansion: Likes and Dislikes

A Read the sentences and write the verbs in bold in the table.

1. I **like** pink T-shirts. They're pretty.
2. I **hate** my school uniform! It's ugly!
3. I **don't like** the color green.
4. I **love** shopping for clothes. It's fun!

Likes and dislikes	
☺ ☺	
☺	like
☹	
☹ ☹	

B Rewrite sentences 1–4 in **A** and make them true for you. Then tell your partner.

Grammar

Object Pronouns		
Subject Pronouns	Verb	Object Pronouns
I You He She It We They	love(s) like(s) don't / doesn't like hate(s)	**me**. **you**. **him**. **her**. **it**. **us**. **them**.

*I love **these green pants**. → I love **them**.*   *We like **pizza**. → We like **it**.*

C Underline the correct pronoun to complete the sentence.

1. **A:** Do you want this hat? **B:** No, I hate *it* / *them*.
2. I'm looking for a new tie. Can you help *I* / *me*?
3. Your brother is nice. I like *him* / *her*.
4. She wears those shoes every day. She loves *it* / *them*!
5. My favorite color is purple. Do you like *it* / *us*?

The neighborhood of Shibuya in Tokyo, Japan, is a popular place for shopping and fashion.

Conversation

🎧 51 Chung and Brenda are buying a present for Brenda's brother. Listen and read the conversation. What are they buying? Which soccer team does her brother like?

Chung: Does your brother like soccer?

Brenda: Yes, he does. Why?

Chung: Because this store has soccer shirts for famous teams.

Brenda: Great! Let's go in and look at them.

Chung: How about this shirt? I think it's Manchester United.

Brenda: No, he doesn't like them. He loves Juventus.

Chung: OK, so buy him a Juventus shirt. What size is he?

SPEAKING STRATEGY

Make Suggestions
Let's ...
How about ...?
OK, so ...

E Practice the conversation in pairs. Switch roles and practice it again.

F Practice the conversation again. Pick a different present for a person that you know.

✓ GOAL CHECK Express Likes and Dislikes

1. Complete the first column of the chart with things like clothes, food, sports, activities, and places. Check (✓) the columns to show your likes and dislikes.

	☺ ☺ I love ...	☺ I like ...	☹ I don't like ...	☹ ☹ I hate ...
1. jeans				
2. the color red				
3. blue clothes				
4.				
5.				
6.				
7.				
8.				

2. Ask for your partner's opinions about your chart. Write an x in the chart for your partner's answers. Then share your answers with the class.

Do you like strawberry ice cream?

Yes, I love it.

I hate strawberry ice cream, but Rafael loves it.

D GOAL Talk about Personal Qualities

A Look at the photos. What colors are her shirts? Which color do you prefer? Why?

B Read the article. What is the main message?

　　a. It's important to wear different clothes at work.

　　b. Colors can change what people think about us.

　　c. Clothes are more important than colors.

C These people don't know what color to wear. Find the best color in the article.

　　1. "I have an interview for a new job tomorrow!" black

　　2. "My friend is a painter, so I have to meet him at a gallery today."

　　3. "It's my birthday. Let's go to a nightclub!"

　　4. "What a beautiful day! I feel great!"

　　5. "I want to go for a walk in the park."

　　6. "I'm meeting some new people tonight."

D Work in pairs. Answer the two questions at the end of the article. Do you think that color is important? Why?

E Match the adjectives from the article to the sentences.

creative	friendly	helpful
intelligent	interesting	positive

　　1. Stella does well in school. intelligent

　　2. Nick is nice and he loves meeting new people.

　　3. My grandfather tells amazing stories. I love to listen to him.

　　4. They are musicians and they write music.

　　5. Every morning, she's happy and excited.

　　6. Richard is a good sales assistant. He always asks customers, "Can I help you?"

✓ GOAL CHECK

In pairs, describe different people you know using the adjectives in **E**. What colors from the article suit the people best? Give reasons and examples.

> My sister is very creative. She paints and likes to take photos. Purple suits her.

What does the color of your clothes say about you?

When you go to work or school, do you think about the colors of your clothes? You might not, but it's important because people have different feelings when they see different colors. For example, look at this woman. In each photo she's wearing the same shirt, but the colors are different. Which color makes you think she's very professional? Which color is friendly and fun? Which color makes her look interesting?

Psychologists believe that color can change how we feel about a person, so when you choose your clothes, choose the correct color for the correct situation:

Black is a good color for job interviews, because people think you are very professional.

Blue is a friendly color, so when you want to make friends, wear something blue.

Red is good for going out and having fun. Wear red to a party.

Yellow is the color of the sun, and people often wear yellow in the summer. It's a happy and positive color.

Purple makes you look interesting. People think that you are creative and you love art.

Green means you are a helpful person and other people may ask for your help. Maybe you like nature and animals.

So, what color are your clothes today? What do they say about you?

psychologist a person who studies the human mind

GOAL Describe your Favorites

Communication

A Read the directions. Then play the game in small groups.

What's your FAVORITE?!

Go to the START square. Take turns flipping a coin. Move 1 square for heads or 2 squares for tails. Answer the question in the square.

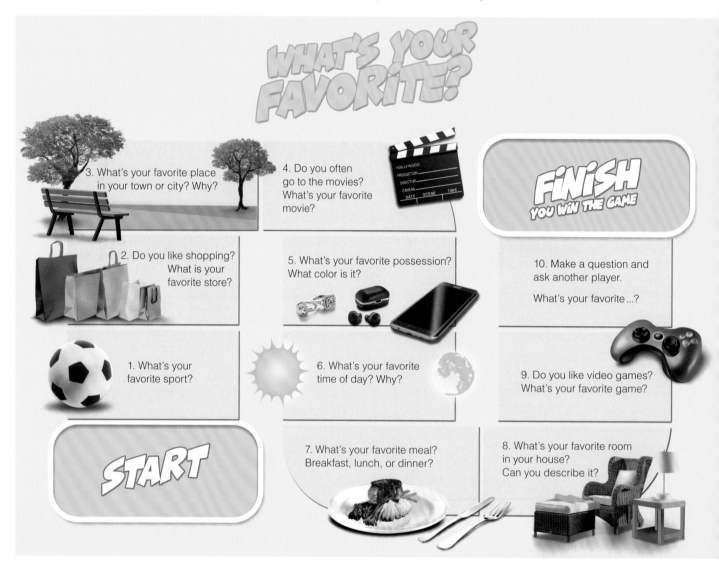

WHAT'S YOUR FAVORITE?

3. What's your favorite place in your town or city? Why?

4. Do you often go to the movies? What's your favorite movie?

FINISH YOU WIN THE GAME

2. Do you like shopping? What is your favorite store?

5. What's your favorite possession? What color is it?

10. Make a question and ask another player. What's your favorite ...?

1. What's your favorite sport?

6. What's your favorite time of day? Why?

9. Do you like video games? What's your favorite game?

START

7. What's your favorite meal? Breakfast, lunch, or dinner?

8. What's your favorite room in your house? Can you describe it?

Writing

B Read a descriptive paragraph. What is the writer's favorite place? What are two of the reasons?

> My favorite place in my town is the local market. It's open on Tuesdays and Saturdays, and I often go with friends. I like it because there are different clothing stalls and the clothes are very cheap. Also, you can eat food there— it's delicious!

The Rot Fai Market in Bangkok, Thailand

C Read about paragraphs. Then underline the topic sentence of the paragraph in **B**.

WRITING SKILL: Paragraphs

A paragraph has one topic sentence and two or three supporting sentences:
1. Start with your topic sentence: *My favorite...is...*
2. Write your reason: *I like it because... | I love it because...*
3. Write another reason: *Also,... | I also like it...*

D Look at the sentences from a paragraph. Put them in the correct order from 1 to 4.

_____ I usually wake up at six o'clock and drink coffee.

_____ My favorite time of the day is the morning.

_____ Also, I can watch the sunrise from my bedroom window—it's beautiful!

_____ It's early, but I love this time of day because it's quiet.

✓ **GOAL CHECK** Describe Your Favorites

1. Choose one of these topics and write a paragraph.
   - favorite clothes
   - favorite sport
   - favorite time of day
   - favorite place
   - favorite possession
   - favorite time of year

2. Exchange paragraphs with a partner. Is there a topic sentence? How many supporting sentences are there?

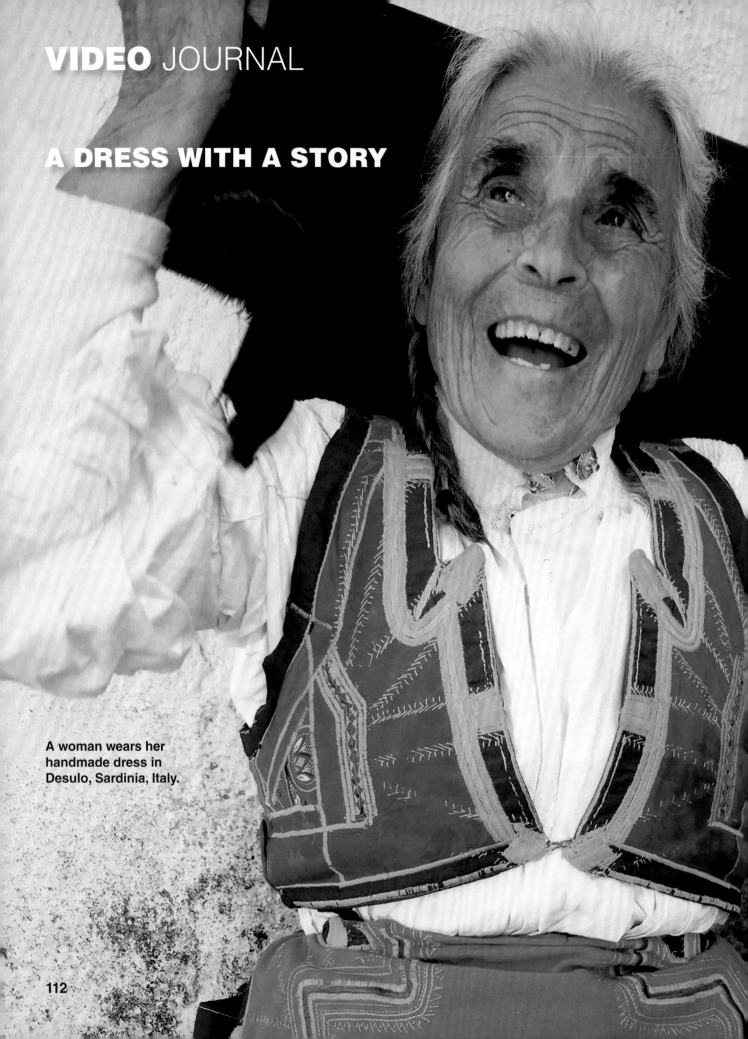

A DRESS WITH A STORY

A woman wears her handmade dress in Desulo, Sardinia, Italy.

A Look at the traditional clothes in the photo. Which country do you think this woman from?

B Does your country have traditional clothes? When do people wear them? What color are they?

C Watch the video. Number the actions in the order you see them.

_____ A woman is looking at old photos of her parents.

_____ Two women are standing together in a red dress and a black dress.

__1__ A woman is sewing her dress with a needle.

_____ A woman is standing in a dress. She also has a black headscarf.

_____ A woman is standing in a red, yellow, blue, and black dress.

_____ A woman is looking at the mountains.

D Read the sentences from the video and underline the correct words.

1. Sardinia is *an island* / *a country* in the Mediterranean Sea.

2. The middle of the island is very *busy* / *quiet*.

3. Desulo is a *city* / *village* in the mountains.

4. Over the years, the women *make a new* / *change their* dress.

5. When they get married, the dress is *red* / *black*.

6. *The old woman* / *The dress* tells the story of a life.

E Watch the video again and check your answers.

F Think of three important objects in your life and write them in this table (e.g., a photo of your parents, a special book).

What is the object?	Why is it important in your life?

G Work in pairs. Take turns describing your three objects.

Kamayan means "by hand" in the Philippines. It refers to eating together with friends and family without plates or utensils.

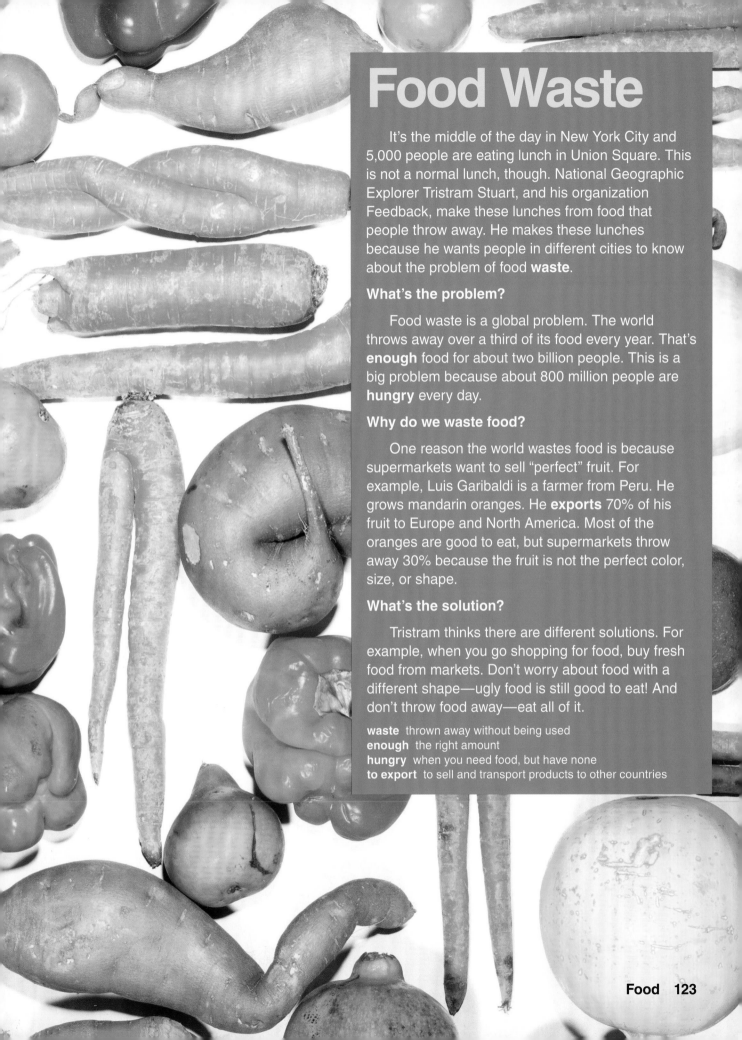

Food Waste

It's the middle of the day in New York City and 5,000 people are eating lunch in Union Square. This is not a normal lunch, though. National Geographic Explorer Tristram Stuart, and his organization Feedback, make these lunches from food that people throw away. He makes these lunches because he wants people in different cities to know about the problem of food **waste**.

What's the problem?

Food waste is a global problem. The world throws away over a third of its food every year. That's **enough** food for about two billion people. This is a big problem because about 800 million people are **hungry** every day.

Why do we waste food?

One reason the world wastes food is because supermarkets want to sell "perfect" fruit. For example, Luis Garibaldi is a farmer from Peru. He grows mandarin oranges. He **exports** 70% of his fruit to Europe and North America. Most of the oranges are good to eat, but supermarkets throw away 30% because the fruit is not the perfect color, size, or shape.

What's the solution?

Tristram thinks there are different solutions. For example, when you go shopping for food, buy fresh food from markets. Don't worry about food with a different shape—ugly food is still good to eat! And don't throw food away—eat all of it.

waste thrown away without being used
enough the right amount
hungry when you need food, but have none
to export to sell and transport products to other countries

A In pairs, think of five examples of healthy foods and five examples of unhealthy foods. Then compare your lists with another pair's.

Healthy	Unhealthy
_____	_____
_____	_____
_____	_____
_____	_____
_____	_____

B Read the "How To" information from a website. What examples does it have of healthy and unhealthy foods?

> **How to Have a Healthy Diet**
> There are lots of ways you can have a healthy diet:
> - Eat five types of fruits and vegetables a day, such as potatoes, carrots, apples, lettuce, and bananas.
> - Over a third of a healthy diet is food like bread, pasta, and rice.
> - Fish is a good example of a healthy food. Eat fish twice a week or more.
> - Don't eat lots of foods and drinks with sugar; for example, candy, soda, and ice cream.
> - Drink about two liters (or a half a gallon) of water every day.

In the US, people spend over $32 billion a year on candy.

Writing

C Read the information. Then underline the words and phrases in **B** for giving examples.

> **WRITING SKILL:** Giving Examples
>
> When we write information, we often give examples:
> - *Eat more green vegetables;* **for example,** *lettuce and broccoli.*
> - *Don't eat fast food,* **such as** *burgers and fries.*
> - *Salad* **is a good example of** *a healthy food.*
> - *For breakfast, I eat food* **like** *cereal, milk, and eggs.*

D Write the missing words in these sentences.

1. Running is a _____ example _____ a healthy exercise.

2. When you study, take regular breaks; for _____, go for a walk.

3. I often play sports, _____ soccer and tennis.

4. The children like desserts, such _____ ice cream and cake.

Communication

E Choose one of these "How To" titles in a small group.

- How to Get More Exercise
- How to Learn More English
- How to Have More Free Time
- How to Make a Healthy Meal

F Discuss your choice in **E**. Write down four or five ways to do it.

✓ GOAL CHECK Explain How to Do Something

Write "How To" information for a website. Use your title from **E** and your ideas from **F**. Try to give examples in your writing.

VIDEO JOURNAL

BERRY ROAD TRIP

A Answer the questions in pairs.

1. Where do you buy your food?

2. Which food is from your country?

3. Which food is from other countries?

B Match the words and symbols to the definitions.

1. lbs _____   3. % _____

2. $ _____   4. mile _____

a. It's a type of distance. It equals 1.6 kilometers.

b. A pound is a type of weight. It is 453 grams.

c. A percentage.

d. A dollar is a type of money.

C MY WORLD Write answers to the questions.

1. How far is it from your school or place of work to your home? _____ miles

2. What is your country's currency? _____

3. How much of your day do you spend at school or work? _____ %

D Watch the video. Number the actions in the order you see them.

| 1 | Lots of trucks are driving in different directions. |

| _____ | The strawberries are in a box. The box is in a case. The case is on a pallet. |

| _____ | The truck is driving across the US from Watsonville, CA to Washington, DC. |

| _____ | A person is buying strawberries from a store. |

| _____ | A man is putting the pallets of strawberries into a truck. |

| _____ | One driver is sleeping. |

E Watch the video again in pairs. Student A answers questions 1–6 and Student B answers questions 7–12.

1. How many trucks are on the road every day? ______
2. On average, how far can food travel before it's in the store? ______ miles
3. How many pounds of strawberries are there per box? ______
4. How many cases are there on a pallet? ______
5. How much do the strawberries on one truck cost? $______
6. How many drivers are there? ______
7. How much of our food do we transport? ______%
8. How many strawberry trucks are there? ______
9. How many pallets are on a truck? ______
10. How much does it cost to put fuel in the truck? $______
11. How long does the trip take? ______ days
12. How many hours can one person drive per day? ______ hours

F Take turns asking your partner their questions. Write down their answers.

G Watch the video again. Are your partner's answers correct?

H Imagine you are making a similar type of video about your life. Write down ten important facts (numbers, percentages, years, etc.). Then work in pairs and tell your partner about your facts.

People compete in an Aquathlon (swimming and running race) in Manaus, Brazil.

A Life-Saving DELIVERY

1   Rwanda is a small country in central East Africa. A lot of its people live in rural areas, and often there aren't good roads to the villages. Because transportation is a problem, doctors in Rwanda often cannot get medicine for their patients. But now they have a high-tech solution.

2   Zipline is a drone service that delivers medicine. Zipline doesn't use cars and trucks. Its drones can quickly deliver medicine over mountains and forests and across rivers. The process is simple. First of all, when a hospital in Rwanda needs medicine, the doctor sends a text message to Zipline. Next, Zipline puts the medicine into a small red box with a parachute. Then, the drone flies to the hospital and, finally, it drops the box to the ground.

3   Zipline's drones are a good example of how technology can be positive and important in our lives. The drones can make 500 deliveries per day, and the average flying time is 30 minutes (by truck it's about 5 hours). The drone can fly almost 50 miles in a trip. As a result, Zipline is also now delivering in Ghana and, in the future, it plans to deliver in other countries, including rural parts of the United States.

E GOAL Describe Healthy Living

Communication

A **MY WORLD** Do you know a person who is old and healthy (e.g., a grandparent)? Why do you think they are healthy?

B Look at this list of activities for a long and healthy life. Which activity do you think is the most important? Which do you think is the least important?

- Get regular exercise
- Eat a lot of fruit and vegetables
- Get 7–8 hours of sleep every night
- Have close friends and face-to-face contact
- Breathe clean air
- Take time to relax

C Work in small groups. Discuss your opinions in **B**.

D Read the text. What is Susan Pinker's answer to **B**? Do you agree with her?

According to psychologist Susan Pinker, there are different activities for a long and healthy life. First, healthy people eat a lot of fruit and vegetables. In addition, they don't smoke, and they also get regular physical exercise. Finally, she thinks that you should have close friends and face-to-face contact—those are the most important things for a long and healthy life.

Spending time with close friends can lead to a long and healthy life. Do you think these women in China will live long lives?

Writing

E Read about sequencing and adding information. Then underline examples of sequencing and adding language in the paragraph in **D**.

> **WRITING SKILL:** Sequencing and Adding Information
>
> When we write information in a paragraph, we often use:
> - **sequencing language:** First, / Second, / Finally,
> - **adding language:** Also, / They also … / In addition,

F Write the missing word in the sentences.

1. To have a healthy heart, people should exercise daily. They should _____ eat a lot of vegetables.

2. A walk in the park is good for your health. _____, it's relaxing to go outside. Second, you get exercise.

3. When you have the flu, you should stay in bed. In _____, you should take medicine.

G Look at a student's plan for a paragraph about mental health. She has four ideas for the topic. Can you think of any more ideas? Add them to the plan.

WRITING STRATEGY

Before you write an information paragraph, it's useful to plan first. One way to plan is to use graphic organizers like the one in **G**.

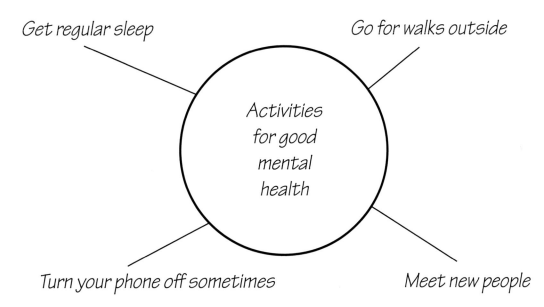

Get regular sleep

Go for walks outside

Activities for good mental health

Turn your phone off sometimes

Meet new people

✓ **GOAL CHECK** Describe Healthy Living

1. Use the plan in **G** and write a paragraph starting with this topic sentence:
   There are different activities for good mental health.

2. Exchange your paragraph with a partner. Does your partner's paragraph use language for sequencing and adding information?

VIDEO JOURNAL

WHAT MAKES YOU HAPPY?

A Look at the photo. How happy are these people? Score them from 0 to 10
(0 = not happy, 10 = happy).

☹   😐   ☺

0 1 2 3 4 5 6 7 8 9 10

B In groups, discuss what makes people happy. Look at the reasons and put them
in order from 1 (most important) to 8 (less important).

_____ Good health   _____ Family and friends

_____ A good economy   _____ Physical exercise

_____ Good schools and education   _____ A green environment

_____ Sunny weather   _____ A job and hard work

C **MY WORLD** What things in **B** make you happy? What else makes you happy?
Tell a partner.

**Families play on the beach at sunset
at Playa Flamingo, Costa Rica.**

140

D Watch the video. Check (✓) the reasons for happiness in each country.

	Costa Rica	Denmark	Singapore
1. Good health	✓		
2. A green environment			
3. A good education			
4. Sunny weather			
5. A good economy			
6. Family and friends			
7. A job and hard work			

E Circle **T** for *true* or **F** for *false*.

1. People from 140 countries answered the poll questions.　　　　　　　T　F

2. Seven or above means you are very happy.　　　　　　　　　　　　T　F

3. People from different countries have similar answers to the questions.　T　F

4. Costa Rica has beautiful beaches.　　　　　　　　　　　　　　　　T　F

5. People don't have much money in Denmark.　　　　　　　　　　　　T　F

6. In most countries, people think physical health is very important.　　　T　F

F Watch the video again and check your answers in **E**.

G In small groups, write seven or eight questions about happiness. For example:
How important is physical exercise? Does sunny weather make you happy?

H Exchange your questions with another group and answer their questions.

People walk down a colorful alley in Athens, Greece.

UNIT 11 GOALS

A. Plan Special Days

B. Describe a National Holiday

C. Make Life Plans

D. Compare Festivals

E. Invite People

A GOAL Plan Special Days

Vocabulary

A Match the special days to the photos. Which days are every year?

an anniversary	a birthday	a graduation
a new job	a new year	a wedding

1. _____

2. _____

3. _____

4. _____

5. _____

6. _____

WORD FOCUS

You can talk about plans with these verbs: *plan to, want to.*
I plan to *have a party for my birthday.*
My parents **want to** *go out for dinner.*

B **MY WORLD** Think about you and your family. Which special days do you plan to celebrate this year?

C In pairs, read about the special days and decide how to celebrate them. Complete the sentences with phrases from the box and your own ideas.

cook a special meal	give a present	go out to eat	go to the movies
have a party	invite family to the house	make a cake	send a card

1. For my best friend's birthday, I always _____.

2. On my mom and dad's anniversary, they always _____.

3. My sister's college graduation is this year. We plan to _____.

4. John has a new job, so tonight we want to _____.

5. Every New Year's Day, I meet friends and we _____.

D Tell a partner what you do on your birthday.

What do you do on your birthday?   I normally ...   This year, I plan to ...

Grammar

Be going to			
Statement	Negative	Yes / No Question	Wh- Question
I **am going to** have a party.	We **are not going to** have a big meal.	**Are** you **going to** go to the movies?	What **is** he **going to** do? When **are** we **going to** go?

*We use *be going to* for making plans.
*We also use these time expressions: *tomorrow, next Saturday / week / year*.

E Complete the conversations. Use *be going to* and the words in parentheses. Then practice the conversations in pairs.

1. **A:** What _____ (you) do for your birthday?

   B: I _____ have a BIG party! People are going to give me presents.

2. **A:** _____ (you) have a barbecue this weekend?

   B: No, we _____ go to the movies.

3. **A:** Where _____ (Courtney and Min) go on New Year's Eve?

   B: They _____ go to Punta Cana and relax on the beach.

F Complete these sentences with your own plans.

1. After class, I'm going to _____.

2. This weekend, I'm going to _____.

3. Next month, I'm going to _____.

G Work in pairs. Use *be going to* to ask your partner questions about their plans in **F**.

> What are you going to do after class?

> I'm going to meet some friends.

> Are you going to go to the movies this weekend?

> No, I'm not. I'm…

✔ GOAL CHECK Plan Special Days

1. In groups, choose a special day. For example, New Year's Eve or a graduation. Decide:

   - what you are going to do.
   - where it is going to be.
   - who you are going to invite.

2. Join another group and present your plans.

On New Year's Eve in New York City, people often celebrate in Times Square. The Chinese New Year is later in the year.

Vocabulary

A 🎧 67 Number the months in the correct order. Then listen and check.

☐ January ☐ July ☐ September ☐ May ☐ December ☐ February

☐ April ☐ October ☐ November ☐ March ☐ June ☐ August

B 🎧 68 Match the dates to the special days and holidays. Then listen and check. Notice how we say the dates.

1. March 3rd _____   **a.** Valentine's Day

2. February 14th _____   **b.** Independence Day in Bolivia

3. April 22nd _____   **c.** Halloween

4. May 1st _____   **d.** Girl's Day in Japan

5. August 6th _____   **e.** Earth Day

6. October 31st _____   **f.** Labor Day (in many countries)

C In pairs, say the dates for these special days.

- Your birthday

- New Year's Day

- Independence Day or a national holiday in your country

Listening

D 🎧 69 Listen to two conversations. Write the dates you hear.

1. New Year's Eve in the US is on _____.

2. This year, the New Year in China starts on _____

3. Independence Day in the US is on _____

4. Independence Day in Brazil is on _____

E 🎧 69 Listen again and answer the questions.

   1. Why isn't Linda going to Times Square?

   2. What is she going to do?

   3. What is Chen going to do?

   4. What is Tom going to do during the day?

   5. What is he going to do at night?

   6. What time is he going to leave?

PRONUNCIATION: *Be going to* (Reduced Form)

In everyday speech, *going to* often sounds like "gunna." This change does not happen in writing.
Full: /goʊɪŋ tu/   Reduced: /gənə/

F 🎧 70 Listen and check (✓) the correct column.

	Full Form	Reduced Form
1. We're going to have a party.	✓	
2. We're going to have a party.		✓
3. I'm going to go to Paris.		
4. I'm going to go to Paris.		
5. They're not going to come.		
6. They're not going to come.		

G Practice the conversations in pairs. Use the reduced form of *be going to*.

   A: What are you going to do this weekend?

   B: I'm going to go to the beach.

   A: Are you going to go to Kim's party?

   B: No, I'm going to stay home on Sunday.

✓ **GOAL CHECK** Describe a National Holiday

Answer the questions in the table with your own information. Then work in groups of three. Ask your classmates the questions and complete the table.

	You	Classmate 1	Classmate 2
What is your favorite holiday in your country?			
What date(s) is it going to be on this year?			
What are you going to do?			

GOAL Make Life Plans

Language Expansion: Professions

A Read about Laura. What is her life plan?

This is Laura. Someday she would like to go to space. She loves science, and she's going to be an astronaut when she graduates from college.

B Match the professions (1–6) to the people (a–f).

1. nurse _____   **2.** lawyer _____   **3.** musician _____

4. software engineer _____   **5.** actor _____   **6.** teacher _____

C **MY WORLD** Put the six professions in **B** in order from most (1) to least (6) interesting. Then compare your ideas in pairs. Do you agree? Why?

Grammar

Would like to for Wishes

Statement	Yes / No Question	Short Answer	Wh- Question
I **would like to** be a nurse. Danny **would like to** study law.	**Would** you **like to** study engineering? **Would** you **like to** be a nurse?	Yes, I **would**. No, I **wouldn't**.	What **would** you **like to** be?

D Write the wishes and plans. Add one of your own.

Wish

1. I would like to be an actor.
2. Leo would like to be a doctor.
3. _____
4. We would like to see the fireworks.
5. _____
6. _____

Plan

I am going to study acting.

_____

I am going to study information technology.

_____

They are going to study music.

_____

Conversation

E 🎧 71 Listen to the conversation. What would Carol like to be? How is she going to do it?

Father: So, Carol, you're <u>18 years old</u> today. What are you going to do with your life?

Carol: I'd like to get married and have children.

Father: What? Not so fast!

Carol: Just kidding! I'd like to <u>become a lawyer</u>.

Father: Really?

Carol: Yes, seriously. I'm going to <u>study law in college</u>.

SPEAKING STRATEGY

Being Serious and Not Serious
Being serious: *I'm serious. / I'm not joking. / Seriously!*
Not being serious: *Just kidding! / I'm joking!*

F Practice the conversation in pairs. Switch roles and practice it again.

G Change the underlined words and make a new conversation.

✓ **GOAL CHECK** Make Life Plans

1. Answer the questions.
   • What would you like to be in the future? (e.g., a doctor)
   • How are you going to do it? (e.g., go to college, work in a hospital)

2. Work in groups. Tell each other about your life plans.

D GOAL Compare Festivals

A Do you have these four seasons in your country? Which months are in each season?

> spring   summer   fall   winter

B Read the article. Which festival is in...

March? _____

April? _____

May? _____

C Match the words from the article to their definition.

1. ancient _____   **a.** a lot of different colors

2. colorful _____   **b.** very old

3. beautiful _____   **c.** large groups of people

4. crowds _____   **d.** nice to look at

D Read the article again. Check (✓) the sentences that are true for each festival.

	Las Mayas	Cherry Blossom	Holi
1. It's in the spring.	✓	✓	✓
2. It's always on the same date.			
3. It's more than one day.			
4. Flowers are very important.			
5. The festival has many colors.			
6. There are large crowds.			
7. There is music at the festival.			
8. It is in one country.			

E Compare the three festivals in pairs.

1. What is similar about the festivals? What is different?

2. Which festival would you like to go to? Why?

✓ GOAL CHECK

1. Think of a festival in your country. Make notes about...
- its time of year / dates.
- its length (one day? a week?).
- what people can see at the festival.
- what is most important. Music? Color? Flowers?

2. Work in groups. Describe and compare your festivals. What is similar? What is different?

Spring Festivals

After a long, dark winter, everyone feels happy when it's spring. So, many people around the world plan festivals to celebrate the beginning of this season.

Festival of Las Mayas: Spain

Every year on May 2nd, there is a festival in the town of Colmenar Viejo. "Las Mayas" is an ancient festival. Local families make **altars** with colorful flowers. On each altar, a girl between the ages of 7 and 11 years old sits in a beautiful dress for two hours. Bands play music and crowds of people walk past.

The Cherry Blossom Festival: Japan

Cherry blossoms are Japan's national flower, so Japanese people celebrate them with a festival in the spring. In April, people come to look at the

beautiful, pink flowers. In the afternoons and evenings, they sit under the trees with friends and enjoy food, drinks, and music.

Holi: India and Nepal

Around the middle of March, people in India and Nepal celebrate the **arrival** of spring. The festival lasts for one night and one day. People sing and dance around fires at night. Then, the next day, hundreds of people throw different-colored powders and water at each other.

altar a platform or table, for religion
arrival the time when something begins

A girl sits on her altar during Las Mayas.

Writing

A Do you ever give or receive invitations? What are the invitations for?

B Read the three invitations. Which invitations are to one person? Which is an invitation to a lot of people?

Dear Laura,

My parents are going to celebrate their 25th Wedding Anniversary on March 27th. The family would like to invite you to this special day. The celebration is going to be at our house and starts at 6 pm. Looking forward to hearing from you.

Best wishes,
Ana

Hi!

I'm going to go out for dinner after my graduation on April 18th. I'm going out with friends. Would you like to come? We're going to meet outside the school at 7.

Bye!

Summer Festival
This summer, our town is going to be 200 years old! Come and celebrate this anniversary at 2 pm on Saturday, August 1st, in the park. There's going to be music, dancing, food, and drinks. Everyone is welcome!

People watching fireworks in Montreal, Canada, for the city's 375th anniversary. Many cities have celebrations or festivals on anniversaries.

C Read the invitations again and make notes in the table.

What is it?	Wedding Anniversary		
Date?			
Time?			
Place?			
Any other information? (e.g., music, food)			

D Read about more and less formal writing. Then underline examples of more and less formal writing in the three invitations. Which invitation is the most formal?

WRITING SKILL: More Formal and Less Formal Writing

More formal writing	**Less formal writing**
• We often use: *Dear...* and *Best wishes* • We normally use complete sentences with no contracted forms: *I would like to invite you to... / We are going to...* • We don't use exclamation points.	• We use: *Hi!* and *Bye!* • We often use short sentences with contracted forms: *I'd like to invite you... / We're going to...* • We often use exclamation points.

Communication

E Work in groups. Choose one of the situations. Discuss your plans and make notes in the table.

- Your school is fifty years old this year. Plan an anniversary celebration.
- Your company is seventy-five years old. Plan an anniversary party for the staff.
- Your town is three hundred years old. Plan a weekend of activities in the local park.

What is the event?	
When is it?	
At what time?	
Where is it?	
Other information? (e.g., music, food)	

✓ GOAL CHECK Invite People

1. Decide how you are going to invite people to your event in **E** (a letter, an email, an ad, etc.). Write an invitation using your notes in the table.

2. Exchange invitations in pairs. How formal is your partner's invitation?

VIDEO JOURNAL

CATCHING A HUMMINGBIRD

A Do you ever take photos? Do you photograph animals such as birds?

B Read about hummingbirds and answer these questions.

1. How big are they?
2. Why are they intelligent?
3. Why is it difficult to see them?
4. How can scientists study hummingbirds?

C Watch the first part of the video and answer the questions.

1. Who is Anand Varma?
2. What would he like to do for this project?
3. Does he need a special camera for this project?

D Underline the correct word. Then watch again to check your answers.

1. Anand often works with *other photographers / scientists*.
2. Taking photographs of animals is *easy / difficult*.
3. Anand *needs to / doesn't need to* plan each photograph.
4. First, he's going to prepare his *studio / office*.
5. Nowadays, cameras are much better than in the *past / present*.
6. The *rain / fog* machine shows how a hummingbird moves.
7. The hummingbird is in a *plastic / metal* box with rain.

E Watch the second part of the video. Number the actions in the order you see them.

The hummingbird is flying through fog.

The hummingbird is using its forked tongue.

Rain is falling on the hummingbird.

The hummingbird is shaking the water off itself.

F What adjectives describe hummingbirds? Make a list. Compare your ideas in pairs.

> Hummingbirds are very small. Most are about 3–5 inches long. They are intelligent because their brain is big for their size. And they are very fast, so it's difficult to see them. But now, using special cameras, scientists can study how hummingbirds move.

G In pairs, think of an animal or natural place in your country. Make a plan to photograph and video the animal or place.

• Why do you want to photograph this animal or place?

• What are you going to take with you? Make a list of items.

• When are you going to do this?

H Join another pair and tell them about your plans in **G**.

Kristina Khudi and her family are part of the Nenets people of the Siberian Arctic in Russia. The Nenets live in tents and move 800 miles a year with their reindeer.

UNIT 12 GOALS

A. Talk about Your Past

B. Ask about the Past

C. Describe a Vacation

D. Compare the Past and Present

E. Give Biographical Information

A

GOAL Talk about Your Past

Vocabulary

A Match the verbs in the box to the photos.

> arrive   get   go   leave   live   move   return   stay   visit

1. _____ in a city

2. _____ to work

3. _____ at a hotel

4. _____ to a new house

5. _____ from a trip

6. _____ at the station

7. _____ home

8. _____ my friends

9. _____ home from work

B Circle the correct verb.

1. The train from Seoul *arrives* / *stays* here at midnight.

2. Phil is leaving Boston and he's *moving* / *arriving* to New York this week.

3. How long are you *going* / *staying* at this hotel?

4. Children *go* / *visit* to school at eight o'clock in the morning.

5. When does Marta *go* / *return* from her vacation in Brazil?

6. On the weekends, I always *visit* / *leave* my grandparents for dinner.

C Write a verb to complete the questions. Then ask and answer the questions in pairs.

1. Where do you _____*live*____?

2. When do you _____ to school / work in the morning? When do you _____ home?

3. When you go on vacation, where do you normally _____? In a hotel?

Grammar

D Compare the sentences. Which is about the present? Which is about the past?

1. Last year, I left San Francisco and I moved to Tokyo.

2. Now, I live in an apartment and I work in Mexico City.

Simple Past		
Regular Verbs	Irregular Verbs	*was / were*
I **worked** in New York. / I **didn't work** in Tokyo. She **lived** in London. / She **didn't live** in Berlin.	You **went** to Mexico City. / You **didn't go** to Buenos Aires. He **got** home at nine. / He **didn't get** home at ten.	I **was** born in 1999. / I **wasn't** born in 2000. They **were** born in Beijing. / They **weren't** born in Shanghai.
Add -ed to regular verbs. Use didn't + base form for the negative.	*See list of irregular verbs on page 185.*	*The verb to be has two past forms: (I/he/she/it) was and (you/we/they) were.*

E Complete the sentences with the simple past of the verb in parentheses.

1. My family and I _____ (move) to a new city last year.

2. Last night, I _____ (not go) to my English class. I visited a friend.

3. In Mongolia, my brother _____ (stay) in a tent for one month.

4. My mother _____ (live) in Rome for two years.

5. He _____ (leave) at 9 o'clock this morning.

F 🎧 73 Complete the information about two famous people who moved to different countries. Write the verbs in the simple past. Then listen and check.

be	go	live	move

Albert Einstein (1) ___*was*___ born in Germany in 1879. In 1895, he

(2) _____ to school in Switzerland. After college, he (3) _____

in Switzerland for 28 years, and then he (4) _____ to the US in 1933.

leave	move	not stay	return

When she was 12, Salma Hayek (5) _____ Mexico and went to school in the

US. A few years later, she (6) _____ to Mexico and became an actress.

But Salma (7) _____ in Mexico. In 1991, she (8) _____ to Hollywood

and became famous around the world.

REAL LANGUAGE

We often use these time expressions with the simple past.

*I was born **in 2002**.*
Last year, *she moved to Beijing.*
They stayed in Mexico **for seven days**.
Yesterday, *I went to the movies.*

WORD FOCUS

Say years like this:
1879 = *eighteen seventy-nine*
2001 = *two thousand and one*
2019 = *two thousand nineteen*

✓ GOAL CHECK Talk about Your Past

1. Choose three important years in your life. Write each year and what happened.

2. Work in pairs. Tell your partner an important year, but do not say why it's important. Your partner guesses the reason.

> In 1999, you were born.

> No.

> You went to your first school.

> Yes, correct!

GOAL Ask about the Past

Listening

A 🎧 74 Listen to an interview with Dr. Chris Thornton. Underline the correct words in his profile.

Name	Chris Thornton
Current city	(1) *Washington, DC* / *New York City*
Place of birth	(2) *Washington, DC* / *New York City*
Subject studied in college	(3) *Archaeology* / *Art history*
Countries worked in	(4) *South Africa* / *Peru* Hungary Cyprus Iran Oman
Work in Oman	He studied the (5) *buildings* / *language* and objects of (6) *ancient* / *modern* people.

B 🎧 75 Read the information and listen to the verbs from the interview. Check (✓) the correct column.

	/d/	/t/	/ɪd/
1. traveled			
2. visited			
3. wanted			
4. studied			
5. worked			
6. liked			

PRONUNCIATION: *-ed* Endings

When simple past verbs end in *-ed*, they can have three ending sounds: /d/ (moved), /t/ (talked), or /ɪd/ (started).

C 🎧 76 In pairs, practice saying the sentences. Then listen and check the *-ed* sounds.

1. Last year, I traveled to Brazil.

2. We wanted to go out last night.

3. They studied English in school.

4. You lived in Wuhan.

5. I worked there in 2015.

6. We liked all the food.

Dr. Chris Thornton is the director of the ancient site of Bat in Oman.

Grammar

Simple Past Questions	
Was / Were	Short Answers
Was he **born** in 2001? **Were** they **born** in the US?	Yes, he **was**. / No, he **wasn't**. Yes, they **were**. / No, they **weren't**.
Wh- Questions	Short Answers
Where **did** you **live**? When **did** you **study** archaeology? How long **did** you **stay** in the country?	In Muscat. In 2005. Six months.

D 🎧 74 Write the missing words to complete the simple past questions and answers. Then listen to the interview with Chris again and check your answers.

1. **A:** _____ you born here?

   B: No, I _____. I _____ born in New York City.

2. **A:** _____ _____ you leave home?

   B: In 1997.

3. **A:** _____ _____ you work?

   B: I _____ in South Africa, Hungary, Cyprus, Iran, and Oman.

4. **A:** _____ _____ you _____ to Oman?

   B: From 2007 to 2015, I went to Oman every winter.

5. **A:** _____ _____ you do there?

   B: We _____ the buildings and objects of ancient people.

Communication

E In pairs, look at the information about Albert Einstein and Salma Hayek in Lesson A.

Student A: Write four simple past questions about Albert Einstein.

Student B: Write four simple past questions about Salma Hayek.

Take turns asking and answering your questions.

✓ GOAL CHECK Ask about the Past

1. Write a list of simple past questions. Use these words and your own ideas.

When / born?	When / leave?	What subjects / study?
Where / born?	Where / move to?	When / go to college?
Where / your family live?	What school / go to?	What / do there?

2. Interview a partner about his or her past. Write down his or her answers.

3. Work with a different partner. Use your notes from 2 and describe your first partner's past.

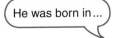

He was born in …   Her family moved in …

GOAL Describe a Vacation

Language Expansion: Going on Vacation

A Look at the phrases and think about your last vacation. Check (✓) the actions you did. Put an (✗) on the actions you didn't do.

take a bus

get a passport

eat out

buy tickets

pack your bag

go to the beach

stay with family or friends

buy sunglasses

WORD FOCUS

Note these irregular simple past forms:
buy – bought
eat – ate
get – got
go – went
take – took

B In pairs, say the actions in **A** that you did or didn't do. Use the simple past. Then make a list of other things you did on your last vacation and tell your partner.

> I took a bus to Samaná.

> I didn't stay with family. I stayed in a hotel.

Grammar

Simple Past	
Yes / No Questions	Short Answers
Did you **buy** the tickets? **Did** she **get** a new passport? **Did** they **go** to the beach?	Yes, I **did.** / No, I **didn't.** Yes, she **did.** / No, she **didn't.** Yes, they **did.** / No, they **didn't.**

C Complete the sentences.

1. **A:** _____ take a train? **B:** Yes, I did.

2. **A:** Did you _____ in a hotel? **B:** No, I didn't. I stayed with friends.

3. **A:** Did _____ a new passport? **B:** No, I _____. I already had one.

4. **A:** Did _____ take a plane? **B:** No, they _____. They took a bus.

5. **A:** _____ buy tickets? **B:** No, she _____.

D In pairs, ask *Yes / No* questions about your partner's last vacation using the phrases in **A**.

Did you eat out?

No, I didn't. It was expensive.

Did you buy new sunglasses?

Yes, I did! And I bought a new hat.

Conversation

E 🎧 77 Listen to the conversation. Where did Liana go on vacation? Did she have a good time?

SPEAKING STRATEGY

David: Hi, Liana! How was your vacation? Did you have a good time?

Liana: <u>Yes, I did</u>. It was <u>so relaxing!</u>

David: Where did you go?

Liana: <u>To Bali.</u>

David: Great! Was it <u>hot</u>?

Liana: <u>Yes, it was, so we went to the beach every day!</u>

David: Was the food good? Did you eat out?

Liana: <u>It was very good. We ate at the night markets a lot. The restaurants were good, too!</u>

Checking Information
Did you ...?
Was it ...?
Were there ...?

F Practice the conversation in pairs. Switch roles and practice it again.

G Change the underlined words and make a new conversation.

✔ GOAL CHECK Describe a Vacation

1. Prepare a short description of your last vacation using some of these phrases and your own ideas.

   • For my last vacation, I went to ...
   • I went with ...
   • We traveled by ...
   • We stayed ...
   • Every day, we ...
   • My favorite part of the vacation was ...

2. In pairs, take turns describing your vacation. Then ask your partner follow-up questions about his or her vacation.

We went to Krabi. We stayed with my grandparents.

Was it ...?

Did you ...?

D GOAL Compare the Past and Present

A Look at the words. Which things do you normally see in the city? Which don't you normally see in the city?

birds	busy traffic	fields	garbage cans
lots of people	skyscrapers	streets	wild animals

B Look at the photo. Where is Mumbai? Why do you think the leopard is walking in the city? Discuss in pairs. Read the article and check your answers.

C Read the article again. Which sentences were true in the past? Which are true in the present.

1. Four billion people live in cities.   **Past**   **Present**

2. Wild animals had to move because cities grew.   **Past**   **Present**

3. There are fewer rural areas.   **Past**   **Present**

4. Some wild animals learn to live in cities.   **Past**   **Present**

5. People believed that wild animals only lived in the countryside.   **Past**   **Present**

D **MY WORLD** Answer the question at the end of the article. Tell the class your answer.

GOAL CHECK

1. Discuss each topic in groups. Write one or two sentences for each topic that compare the past and the present.

   - Transportation
   - School
   - Work and free time
   - Food and health
   - Animals and the environment

   Example:

   Transportation: In the past, people walked and rode bikes to work. Now, most people drive cars or take public transportation.

2. Join another group and compare your ideas for each of the topics.

Humans and Animals on the Move

In the last century, more and more people moved to cities. By 2005, more people lived in cities than outside of them. Today, over four billion people live in cities. That's about 55% of the world's population! And experts think the numbers will grow in the future.

As cities grew in the last century, most wild animals had to move further away into more **rural** areas. But now that is changing. There are fewer **rural** areas left, so as modern cities are growing, some animals are learning to live in the city **instead of** moving away. Take this leopard (see photo). She is living in Mumbai, India, one of the biggest cities in the world!

Like other cities around the world, Mumbai is a busy, noisy place. It doesn't look like a safe place for wild animals, but it is home for many **species**. After all, there is free food in the garbage cans, and tall buildings are good homes for birds. And late at night, when we are sleeping, animals can move freely around our streets.

We once believed that wild animals only lived in the countryside. Now we know that isn't true. So, what animals are living near you?

rural in the country, outside of cities and towns
instead of as a replacement for something
species types of animals

Leopards live in Sanjay Gandhi National Park in Mumbai, India.

GOAL Give Biographical Information

Communication

A Play a guessing game. Follow these rules:

1. Work in teams. Each team writes five sentences about a famous place or person.

2. Join another team. Read your first sentence. The other team guesses the answer. If the other team guesses correctly after the first sentence, they win 5 points. If they guess incorrectly, read the next sentence (and the other team can win 4 points). Keep reading sentences until the other team guesses the answer. Take away 1 point for each new sentence.

3. Each team joins a new team and repeats the game. Try to play with all the teams in your class and win the most points!

Writing

B A student is going to write a short biography about the woman in the photo. Read the student's notes about the woman's life.

<u>Mae C. Jemison</u>, First African American woman in space

<u>October 17, 1956:</u> was born

<u>1959:</u> her family moved to Chicago

<u>Age 16:</u> won a scholarship and went to Stanford University—Wanted to be a scientist. Studied chemical engineering

<u>1981:</u> became a Doctor of Medicine

<u>1987:</u> became a NASA astronaut

<u>September 12, 1992:</u> flew to space on the Endeavor space shuttle

<u>September 20, 1992:</u> returned to Earth

<u>March, 1993:</u> left NASA

<u>Today:</u> has her own company

C Read about time expressions and linking words. Then complete the student's biography using time expressions and linking words from the box.

WRITING SKILL: Time Expressions and Linking Words

When you write about the past, you can use these time expressions and linking words:
*   **Time expressions:** In 1966, ... / In the twentieth century, ... / On May 1st, 2001, ...
*   **Two events at the same time:** When ... / During ... / At that time, ... / At the same time, ...
*   **One event after another:** Later, ... / Then, ... / After that, ... / Next, ...

| after | at that time | eight days later | in 1987 |
| later | ~~three years later~~ | when she was sixteen | |

Mae C. Jemison was the first African American woman in space. She was born on October 17, 1956. (1) *Three years later*, her family moved to Chicago. (2) _____, she won a scholarship and went to Stanford University. (3) _____, she wanted to be a scientist and she studied chemical engineering. (4) _____, in 1981, she became a Doctor of Medicine. Mae also had another dream, and (5) _____, she became a NASA astronaut. (6) _____ years of training, Mae flew into space on the Endeavor space shuttle on September 12, 1992, and (7) _____, she returned to Earth. She left NASA in 1993, and today she has her own company.

Mae C. Jemison was the first African American woman in space.

 You are going to write a biography:

1. Choose a famous person or someone you know well.

2. Think about what information you need about the person.

3. Where can you find the information? Check (✓) the places below.

    1. Interview the person ☐

    2. Read books about history ☐

    3. Look at old photographs ☐

    4. Read newspaper or magazine articles ☐

    5. Watch videos and movies ☐

    6. Search the internet ☐

    7. Interview other people (e.g., someone who knows the person) ☐

    8. What other ways? _____

E Tell a partner about your answers in **D**.

✓ GOAL CHECK Give Biographical Information

1. Take notes about your person and write the biography.

2. Exchange your biography with a partner and read theirs. Did your partner use time expressions and linking words?

VIDEO JOURNAL

LEAVING ANTARCTICA

A Look at the photograph of Antarctica. Say three words to describe it.

B Work in pairs. Can you answer these questions about Antarctica?

1. Is Antarctica a country or a continent?

2. Is the North Pole or South Pole there?

3. Is it smaller or bigger than Australia?

C Watch the video. Check (✓) the things you see.

1. ☐ Dion Poncett in a house

2. ☐ Dion when he was 11 years old

3. ☐ Dion and his brothers in the snow

4. ☐ Boys on a ship and a whale in the ocean

5. ☐ Dion with his mother

6. ☐ Lots of other people

7. ☐ Some land with no snow

8. ☐ A fishing ship

9. ☐ A ship with tourists

Melting ice off the coast of Antarctica

D Watch the video again. Underline the correct verbs.

1. Dion <u>was</u> / *wasn't* born in Antarctica.

2. His father *was* / *wasn't* French.

3. Dion's mother *was* / *wasn't* French.

4. His parents *had* / *didn't have* three daughters.

5. Their three sons *grew up* / *didn't grow up* in Antarctica.

6. Dion *went* / *didn't go* to school.

7. Sally Poncet *was* / *wasn't* a scientist.

8. She *studied* / *didn't study* birds.

9. In 2018, Dion *sold* / *didn't sell* his boat.

E Work in pairs. Student A is a journalist and Student B is Dion. Ask and answer the questions using information from the video.

1. Where did you grow up?

2. What did your parents do?

3. Did you go to school?

4. Why do you love Antarctica?

5. Why did you sell your boat and move away?

6. How do you feel about the changes in Antarctica? Is it important to stop these changes?

F Work in groups. You are going to make a video about the past in your town or city.

Discuss and make notes about:

• which old buildings and places you can show in the video.

• who you can interview about the past. Write five questions for them.

• which changes you can show in the video (e.g., new buildings, more people).

Work with another group and present your plans for the video.

Grammar Reference

UNIT 1

Lesson A

Present Tense of be

Subject Pronoun	Be	
I	**am**	Sam.
You	**are**	
He / She / It	**is**	
We	**are**	Sam and Sara.
They	**are**	

Contractions with be

I**'m**	Sam.
You**'re**	
He**'s** / She**'s** / It**'s**	
We**'re**	Sam and Sara.
They**'re**	

Possessive Adjectives

My	name is	Sam.
Your	name is	Sara.
His	name is	Alex.
Her	name is	Ana.
Its	name is	Max.
Our	names are	Yuki and Laura.
Their	names are	Alex and Ana.

A Underline the correct form of *be*.

1. I *am* / *is* a teacher.
2. She *is* / *are* a teacher.
3. We *is* / *are* teachers.
4. They *am* / *are* students.
5. This *am* / *is* my friend, Julia.

B Write the sentences with contractions.

1. He is Ruben. He's Ruben.
2. I am Diego. _____
3. You are Rebecca. _____
4. They are Ahmet and Omar.

   _____

C Write the possessive adjectives to complete the conversation

Jill: Pleased to meet you. (1) _____ name's Jill.

Ellie: Hi, I'm Ellie.

Jill: Are you here with friends?

Ellie: Yes, I'm with two friends. (2) _____ names are Hussein and Lucas. And you?

Jill: I'm with my husband. (3) _____ name is Jose.

Lesson C

Be + Adjective

Subject	Be	Adjective
I	**am**	single.
You	**are**	tall.
He	**is**	handsome.
She	**is**	young and short.
We	**are**	married.
They	**are**	old.

Questions with *be*			Short Answers	
Are	you	married?	Yes, I **am**.	No, I**'m not**.
Is	he / she / it	old?	Yes, he / she / it **is**.	No, he / she / it **isn't**. No, he / she / it **is not**.
Are	they	tall?	Yes, they **are**.	No, they**'re not**. No, they **aren't**.

*With *yes* short answers, don't use contractions:
Yes, I am. ~~Yes, I'm.~~
Yes, she is. ~~Yes, she's.~~

D Write the correct form of *be*, and the opposite adjective.

1. I'm tall and my friend ___is short___.
2. They're young and we _____.
3. She's single and he _____.
4. Bill is short with long hair and Sheila _____ with _____ hair.

E Complete the conversation. Use contractions where possible.

A: Hi! How's it going?

B: Great! And you?

A: I'm fine. Are you here with Carol?

B: No, I (1) _____. Carol is at home.

A: (2) _____ you and Carol married now?

B: Yes, we (3) _____. Are you and Nigel married?

A: No, we (4) _____.

B: Is Nigel here?

A: No, he (5) _____. I'm here with a friend.

UNIT 2

Lesson A

Negative Present of be		
Subject Pronoun	be + not	
I	**am not**	
You / We / They	**are not**	from Peru.
He / She / It	**is not**	

Contractions with be + not			
I'm not			
You / We / They **aren't**	OR	You**'re** / We**'re** / They**'re not**	from China.
He / She / It **isn't**		He**'s** / She**'s** / It**'s not**	

A Write these sentences with contractions.

1. I am not married. _I'm not married._
2. We are not from Egypt. _____
3. It is not a big country. _____
4. They are not 50 years old. _____
5. He is not a grandfather. _____

B Write the negative present form of *be*. Use contractions.

1. **A:** Is Fatima an artist?

   B: No, she _____.

2. **A:** Are David and Maria married?

   B: No, they _____.

3. **A:** Are you single?

   B: No, I _____.

4. **A:** Is this car from Spain?

   B: No, it _____.

Indefinite Articles (a / an)

We often use *a* / *an* with a person's job or occupation:
a *teacher*, **a** *student*, **an** *artist*, **an** *engineer*

- Use *a* before a word starting with a consonant sound:
  a <u>t</u>eacher, **a** <u>s</u>tudent

- Use *an* before a word starting with a vowel sound:
  an <u>a</u>rtist, **an** <u>e</u>ngineer

- Don't use *a* / *an* with plurals:
  teachers (not ~~a teachers~~)

C Write *a*, *an*, or – (no article).

1. He's _____ waiter.
2. She's _____ musician.
3. Bill is _____ engineer.
4. Sue is _____ artist.
5. They're _____ architects.
6. Nigella and Vanessa are _____ students.
7. I'm _____ nurse.
8. Aran is _____ architect.
9. We're _____ taxi drivers.
10. I'm not _____ student, I'm _____ teacher.

Lesson C

Be + Adjective + Noun		
Statements		
Subject + be	Adjective	Noun
China **is**	a big	country.
Africa and Asia **are**	big	continents.
Microsoft **isn't**	a small	company.
Amazon and Alibaba **aren't**	small	companies.
*The article comes before the adjective in singular sentences.		

Questions				Answers
Be	Subject	Adjective	Noun	
Is	China	a big	country?	Yes, it **is**.
Are	Africa and Asia	big	continents?	Yes, they **are**.
Is	Microsoft	a small	company?	No, it **isn't**.
Are	Amazon and Alibaba	small	companies?	No, they **aren't**.

D Unscramble the sentences and questions.

1. China / Is / a / country? / big

   _____

2. big / The / is / a / country. / United States

   _____

3. is / a / Russia / country. / cold

_____

4. Is / hot / Saudi Arabia / a / country?

_____

5. country? / small / Belize / Is / a

_____

E Answer the questions.

1. Is Mexico a cold country?
No, it isn't. It's a hot country.

2. Is Chile a big country?

_____

3. Is Vietnam a hot country?

_____

4. Is the UK a small country?

_____

5. Is Egypt a wet country?

_____

UNIT 3

Lesson A

There is / There are		
Statement	Question	Answers
There is a bathroom.	**Is there** a bathroom?	Yes, **there is.** No, **there isn't.**
There are two bathrooms.	**Are there** two bathrooms?	Yes, **there are.** No, **there aren't.**

A Write the correct form of _be_ to complete the conversation.

My apartment is small. There (1) _____ four rooms. There (2) _____ a kitchen with a table and four chairs. There (3) _____ a living room with a sofa and a TV. There (4) _____ two bedrooms and there (5) _____ a bathroom between them. The apartment is on the tenth floor. There (6) _____ a balcony, but there are a lot of windows.

B Use the words to write questions about somebody's house.

1. bathroom / upstairs
Is there a bathroom upstairs?

_____

2. swimming pool / backyard

_____

3. stairs / your house

_____

4. garden / front yard

_____

5. three bedrooms / your house

_____

6. closet / bedroom

_____

Singular Nouns	Plural Nouns
1 house 1 bathroom	2 houses 2 bathrooms
With most nouns, add _-s_ at the end of the word to make it plural: house → house**s** bedroom → bedroom**s** With some nouns ending with the letters _s_, _y_, and _o_, add _-es_. With nouns that end in _y_, we also replace the _y_ with an _i_. bus → bus**es** city → cit**ies** potato → potato**es** Some plural nouns are irregular: man → men child → children person → people	

C Write the plural form.

1. apartment _____

2. teacher _____

3. university _____

4. school _____

5. tomato _____

6. child _____

7. bus _____

8. woman _____

Lesson C

Use prepositions of place to say where a person, object, or place is.

Prepositions of Place

in   on   next to   between   under

D Complete the sentences with a preposition.

1.

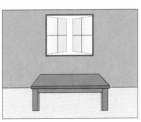

The table is _____ the window.

2.

Your books are _____ my bag.

3.

The sofa is _____ two chairs.

4.

The lamp is _____ the TV.

5.

Your bag is there. It's _____ the table.

UNIT 4

Lesson A

Demonstratives		
	Singular	Plural
Near	**This** is your pen. Is **this** your dictionary?	**These** are not my books. Are **these** your sunglasses?
Far	**That** is your bag. Is **that** your notebook?	**Those** are not my dogs. Are **those** your bags?
*Use *this* and *these* + noun to talk about things close to the speaker. Use *that* and *those* for things far from the speaker.		

A Match the words to the four pictures.

this pen   that pen   these pens   those pens

1.

_____

2.

_____

3.

_____

4.

_____

B Write *this*, *that*, *these*, or *those* to complete the sentences.

1. There's a red car over there. Is _____ car yours?

2. It's right here. _____ bag is Michael's.

3. Are _____ your books on this bookcase?

4. _____ sunglasses are at my house.

Lesson B

Possessive Adjectives

Subject Pronoun	I	you	he	she	it	we	they
Possessive Adjective	my	your	his	her	its	our	their

*Use possessive adjectives to talk about objects, people, and places.

My name is John.   *Those are* **her** *books.*
What's **your** *name?*   **Our** *house is here.*
That's **his** *car.*   **Their** *daughter is a teacher.*

*Possessive adjectives have only one form for both singular and plural: **his** brother → **his** brothers

C Use possessive adjectives to complete the conversation.

A: What's that?

B: It's a photo of (1) _____my_____ family. This is my sister and (2) _____ husband. They have two children. (3) _____ names are Karina and Juan.

A: Are those (4) _____ parents?

B: Well, that's my mother and that's my stepfather. (5) _____ name is Leon.

Possessive Nouns

Singular Nouns	Plural Nouns
Sheila**'s** car the student**'s** house (one student)	the men**'s** pens the student**s'** house (more than one student)

*Talk about people + possessions with the possessive *'s*.
Add -*'s* to a name: *Jim**'s** house*
With plural nouns ending in *s*, put the apostrophe after the *s*: *my parent**s'** house, the student**s'** books*
*The possessive *'s* is not a contraction of *is*:
Antonio's from Brazil. = Antonio is from Brazil.
This is Antonio's car. = The car is Antonio's possession.

D Put the words in order and add the possessive *'s*.

1. car / Joe / is / old.

   _____

2. Vicky / these / are / pens.

   _____

3. Andrew / birthday / tomorrow. / is

   _____

4. hair / is / Laura / long.

   _____

5. Kate / friends. / Lucas and Chen / are

   _____

6. parents / it / is / my / house.

   _____

Lesson C

Have, Has

Statements	Negative
I / You / We / They **have** a phone. He / She / It **has** food.	I / You / We / They **don't have** a phone. He / She / It does**n't have** food.

Yes / No Questions	Short Answers
Do I / you / we / they **have** a phone? Does he / she / it **have** food?	Yes, I / you / we / they **do**. No, I / you / we / they **don't**. Yes, he / she / it **does**. No, he / she / it **doesn't**.

E Complete the sentences with *have* or *has*.

1. Jaime _____ a new laptop.

2. Do you _____ a cell phone?

3. I don't _____ an interesting book.

4. Does Lee _____ a TV?

5. Sofia _____ sunglasses.

UNIT 5

Lesson A

Simple Present

Use the simple present to talk about:

- daily activities and routines: *Every day, I start work at nine o'clock.*

- permanent situations: *She lives in San Francisco.*

Statement		
I / You / We / They	**start**	work at nine o'clock.
He / She / It	**starts**	

Spelling Rules

- Add -*s* to most verbs after *He / She / It*:
  start → starts, work → works

- Add -*es* after verbs ending with -*s*, -*sh*, or -*ch*: *finish → finishes, watch → watches*

- With verbs that end in -*y*, replace the *y* with an *i* and add -*es*. *study → studies*

Negative			
I / You / We / They	don't	**start**	work at nine o'clock.
He / She / It	doesn't		

Wh- Questions			
What	do	I / you / we / they	**do**?
What time When Where	does	he / she / it	**start** work? **leave** work? **live**?

A Write the verb in the correct form.

1. He _____plays_____ (play) the piano.
2. I ___don't study___ (not study) math.
3. Where _____ they _____ (live)?
4. Mark _____ (watch) TV every day.
5. He _____ (not work) in this office.
6. What time _____ she _____ (finish)?
7. Eliza _____ (study) English in college.
8. They _____ (not commute) on weekends.

B Unscramble the words.

1. get / up / I / at / six thirty.
   I get up at six thirty.
2. does not / at eight o'clock. / Elena / start work
   _____
3. at one thirty. / have lunch / We
   _____
4. morning. / I / every / take a shower
   _____
5. work / finishes / at five o'clock. / Paolo
   _____
6. at night. / starts work / My father
   _____

Time Expressions with the Simple Present		
on + days and dates	*at* + times	*in* + *the* + times of the day
on Sunday(s) **on** weekdays **on** weekends	**at** five o'clock **at** noon / midnight **at** lunchtime **at** night (time)	**in** the morning **in** the afternoon **in** the evening

C Write *on*, *at*, or *in*.

1. The meeting is _____ noon.
2. I work _____ night, so I go to bed _____ the morning.
3. There's a party _____ Saturday.

4. We go to the gym _____ the evening, after work.
5. Do you finish work _____ five o'clock?
6. _____ weekends, he visits his parents.

Lesson C

Simple Present Questions			
Do	I you we they	**live** **like** **have**	in Brazil? soccer? a laptop?
Does	he she it		

Short Answers		
Yes,	I / you / we / they	**do**.
	he / she / it	**does**.
No,	I / you / we / they	**don't**.
	he / she / it	**doesn't**.

D Match the questions to the answers.

1. Do you go to the gym every day? _____
2. Do Luis and Felipe live on the same street? _____
3. Does your mother travel a lot? _____
4. Do they go to bed at ten? _____
5. Does the train leave at nine? _____

a. Yes, they do. Their houses are next to each other.
b. Yes, it does.
c. No, I don't. I go about twice a week.
d. Yes, she does. She often travels to Hong Kong for work.
e. No, they don't.

E Complete the conversation with the correct form of *do*.

A: (1) _____ you live in the city?
B: No, I (2) _____. I live in the countryside. My family has a house there.
A: Oh, (3) _____ you have any children?
B: Yes, two. A boy and a girl.
A: (4) _____ they like it?
B: My daughter (5) _____. She loves the countryside. But my son (6) _____.

Adverbs of Frequency

Use adverbs of frequency to talk about how often you do something.

always = 100%   *I **always** get up at seven o'clock.*

sometimes = 50%   *He **sometimes** eats eggs for breakfast.*

never = 0%   *She **never** goes to bed before midnight.*

Word order and *sometimes*

Usually, the adverb of frequency is between the subject and the verb:

*He **always** / **sometimes** / **never** eats eggs for breakfast.*

You can also put *sometimes* at the beginning or the end of the sentence with no change in meaning:

***Sometimes**, he eats eggs for breakfast.*

*He eats eggs for breakfast **sometimes**.*

F Rewrite the sentences with the adverb of frequency.

1. Every day, he goes to school at nine. (always)
   He always goes to school at nine.

2. She plays soccer once a week or once a month. (sometimes)

3. I don't watch TV. (never)

4. My father gets up at five o'clock on weekdays and weekends. (always)

5. His car is always at the garage. It doesn't work. (never)

Lesson E

Imperatives	
Affirmative	Negative
Turn your phone on.	**Don't run**!
Stop at the red light!	**Don't work** too hard.

*Use the imperative form of a verb to:
   Give instructions: **Turn** the computer **on**. **Turn off** the music.
   Give advice: **Don't work** too hard. **Be** nice to him.
   Give orders: **Stop**! **Go**! **Be quiet**!
   Give directions: **Turn** left. **Go** straight ahead.

G Match 1–5 to a–e.

1. Get up! _____
2. Stop the car! _____
3. Don't play computer games all the time. _____
4. Meet me at 5:00. _____
5. Open your books. _____

a. It's bad for you.
b. And do Exercise F.
c. It's time for school.
d. The light is red.
e. And don't be late!

UNIT 6

Lesson A

Prepositions of Place

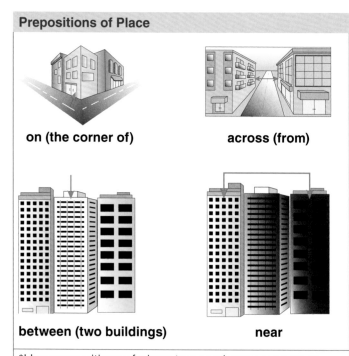

on (the corner of)   **across (from)**

between (two buildings)   **near**

*Use prepositions of place to say where a person or object is.
*Prepositions of place are often after the verb *be*.
*Use *at* with addresses: *It's **at** 100 Washington Avenue.*

A Match the two halves of the sentences.

1. My house is at _____
2. I'm on _____
3. The bank is across _____
4. Your hotel is between _____
5. Is the airport near _____

a. the park and the shopping mall.
b. the corner of Parkwood Road and Coventry Road.
c. here?
d. 51 Parkwood Road.
e. from the library.

Prepositions of Movement

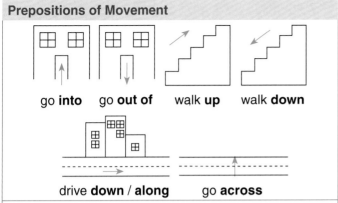

go **into** go **out of** walk **up** walk **down**

drive **down** / **along** go **across**

*Use prepositions of movement to say the direction of movement. Prepositions of movement are used after verbs like *walk*, *run*, *drive*, *move*, *fly*, *go*, and *travel*.

B Write the correct prepositions.

A: How do I get to your office?

B: Go (1) _____ the building and take the elevator. Get (2) _____ the elevator on the fifth floor. Walk (3) _____ the hallway. My office is on the right.

A: How do I get to your school?

B: Turn right at the train station and drive (4) _____ High Street. Drive two blocks and then go (5) _____ Wimbourne Road at the intersection. Drive one more block and my school is on the left. Go in and walk (6) _____ the stairs to the second floor. My classroom is there.

Lesson C

Have to

Statements and Negatives

I You We They	have to don't have to	rent a car.
He She	has to doesn't have to	

*Use *have to* to talk about obligation. Use *don't have to* to talk about no obligation to do something.

Yes / No Questions

Do	I / you / we / they	have to	take a taxi?
Does	he / she		

Short Answers

Yes,	I / you / we / they	do.
	he / she	does.
No,	I / you / we / they	don't.
	he / she	doesn't.

C Underline the correct form of *have to*.

1. Airplane pilots *have to / don't have to* wear uniforms.

2. Drivers in the US *have to / don't have to* drive on the right side of the road.

3. It's free, so Pablo *has to / doesn't have to* pay any money.

4. When you rent a car, you *have to / don't have to* show your driver's license.

5. Yuki *has to / doesn't have to* clean her bedroom. It's messy!

6. *Do / Does* you have to take the subway every day?

D Write sentences using *have to*.

1. Dan doesn't have any money.
   He has to go to the bank.

2. It's 3:00, and your train leaves at 3:30.
   _____

3. Mohamed goes to sleep at 10:00, and it's 9:30.
   _____

4. I have a toothache.
   _____

5. Ann's phone is five years old.
   _____

E Write the correct form of *do* and *have* in these conversations.

1. **A:** You _____ to turn right at the traffic light.

   B: But I _____ to stop because it's red.

   A: Yes, but when it's green, turn right... OK, its green.

2. **A:** OK, you can park here.

   B: _____ we _____ to pay for parking?

   A: No, we _____.

3. **A:** Where's Nigella?

   B: She _____ to work late.

   A: _____ she often _____ to work late?

   B: Yes, she _____.

UNIT 7

Lesson A

Present Continuous

Statements and Negatives

I	'm 'm not	
He / She / It	's isn't	**listening** to music.
You / We / They	're aren't	

*Use the present continuous to talk about actions that are happening at the moment of speaking.

Yes / No Questions

Are	you / they	**working**?
Is	he / she / it	

Short Answers

Yes,	I	**am.**
	he / she / it	**is.**
	you / we / they	**are.**
No,	I	**'m not.**
	he / she / it	**isn't.**
	you / we / they	**aren't.**

Wh- Questions

What	**are**	we / you / they	**doing**?
Where	**is**	he / she / it	**going**?

Spelling Rules

- Most verbs, add -ing to the end: play → playing, go → going, watch → watching
- Verbs ending in a consonant + e: have → having, come → coming
- Double the final consonant on some verbs: shop → shopping, run → running, swim → swimming

A Write the verb in the present continuous.

1. We _____ (go) to the movies.
2. She _____ (play) the guitar.
3. I _____ (run) for the bus!
4. Michael _____ (cook) dinner.
5. I _____ (not sleep). I'm awake.
6. Lucia _____ (not work) this week. She's on vacation.
7. They _____ (not take) a taxi. It's too expensive.
8. It _____ (not rain). It's sunny.

B Write the correct form of be.

A: Hi, (1) _____ you coming?

B: Where are you?

A: I (2) _____ standing outside the movie theater.

B: Oh, no! Sorry, I forgot. I'm doing my homework. My teacher wants it tomorrow. (3) _____ Pedro going as well?

A: No, he (4) _____. He (5)_____ doing his homework, too!

C Make questions in the present continuous.

1. Who / call? _Who's calling?_
2. What / you / do? _____
3. Where / he / go? _____
4. Why / they / shop? _____
5. Dan / play / tennis? _____

D Match these answers to the questions in **C**.

a. They don't have any food. _____
b. Yes, he is. _____
c. It's Christine. _____
d. To the gym. _____
e. I'm watching the soccer game. _____

Lesson C

Can

Can for Ability

Use can to talk about ability: I **can** play soccer. She **can** play tennis very well.

Statement and Negative

I / You / He / She / It / We / They	**can** **can't**	ski.

Can is a modal verb. There is no -s form with he / she / it.
He can ski. ✓
~~He cans ski.~~ ✗

Questions

Can	I / you / he / she / it / we / they	ski?

Short Answers

Yes,	I / you / he / she / it / we / they	**can.**
No,	I / you / he / she / it / we / they	**can't.**

Can for Rules

You can also use can / can't to talk about rules:
You **can** kick the ball. You **can't** use your hands.

Can + Adverbs of Manner

Use *can* + adverbs of manner to talk about how you do something:

> She **can** play the piano (very) **well**.
> He **can** run (very) **fast**.
> **How well can** she play?
> **How fast can** he run?

E Write *can* or *can't* to complete the conversations.

1. **A:** (1) _____ you play the guitar?
   B: No, I (2) _____, but I can sing well.
   (3) _____ you play the song "All You Need Is Love"?
   A: No, sorry, I (4) _____. I don't know it.

2. **A:** What languages (5) _____ you speak?
   B: I (6) _____ speak Chinese, Spanish, and English.
   A: Wow! I can speak English and Spanish, but I (7) _____ speak Chinese.

F Underline the correct words.

1. We can ski, but we *can / can't* skateboard.
2. Yes, I *can / can't*.
3. In soccer, you *can / can't* use your hands.
4. Leo can't swim *very well / not very well*.
5. No, I *can / can't*.
6. In basketball, you *can / can't* kick the ball.

UNIT 8

Lesson A

Can / Could for Polite Requests

Can I try it on, please?	**Could** you pass the salt, please?
Can you repeat that?	**Could** you say that again?
Can I help you?	**Could** you show me another?
Can I have the sugar, please?	**Could** you call me a taxi, please?

*You can use *can* or *could* for polite requests. *Could* is more formal than *can*.
*In English, we often add "please" at the end of the request because it is more polite.
Can and *could* are modal verbs. Do not use the auxiliary verb *do* with modal verbs in questions:
Can you repeat that, please? ✓
~~*Do you can repeat that, please?*~~ ✗

Affirmative Response	Negative Response
Of course. Yes. Sure.	I'm sorry, but… (give reason). I'm afraid that… (give reason).

A Write requests with the words given.

1. Can / try on / this sweater / please?
   _____

2. Could / spell / that / please?
   _____

3. Can / say / that / again?
   _____

4. Could / pass / the / milk, / please?
   _____

5. Can / show / another dress?
   _____

6. Could / have a hamburger / please?
   _____

7. Can / have / cup of coffee / please?
   _____

8. Could / help me?
   _____

B Check (✓) the polite or correct response.

1. Can I try on a blue shirt?
   ☐ No, you can't.   ☐ I'm sorry, but we don't have blue.

2. Could I pay by cash, please?
   ☐ Yes, of course.   ☐ Yes, you do.

3. Can you help me this afternoon?
   ☐ I'm afraid that I'm busy.   ☐ No, I can't.

4. Could you say that again?
   ☐ Yes, sure.   ☐ Yes, course.

Lesson C

Object Pronouns

Subject Pronoun	Verb	Object Pronoun
I		**me.**
You	love(s)	**you.**
He	like(s)	**him.**
She	(don't /	**her.**
It	doesn't) like	**it.**
We	hate(s)	**us.**
They		**them.**

*Object pronouns come after the verb and replace a noun:
*I like **pizza**. → I like **it**.*
*Bill loves **Gill**. → Bill loves **her**.*
*He works with **Chen and Joan**. → He works with **them**.*
*Can you help **me and my friend**? → Can you help **us**?*
*Do you like Rafael? → Do you like **him**?*

C Put the words in the correct order.

1. likes / she / him _____

2. don't / I / them / like _____

3. do / like / you / me? _____

4. my friend / it / hates _____

5. them / are / we / meeting _____

6. doesn't / us / like / Sheila _____

D Complete the conversations with object pronouns.

1. **A:** Do you like your new car?

   B: I love _____!

2. **A:** Can you help _____?

   B: Sure. What's the problem?

3. **A:** Do you know Rachel and Jim?

   B: Yes, I know _____ very well.

4. **A:** I'm walking to the restaurant now. Is Susana meeting _____, too?

   B: Yes, she's already here.

UNIT 9

Lesson A

Some and Any		
Statement	Negative	Question
There's **some** milk in the fridge.	We don't have **any** soda.	Do you have **any** fruit juice?

We use *some* and *any* before a noun to talk about quantities:
*There are **some** onions in the cupboard.* = an amount (e.g., two or more)
*There aren't **any** onions in the cupboard.* = no amount (i.e., zero)

We normally use *some* in positive statements and *any* with negatives and questions. But we can also use *some* with requests with *can / could*:

Can / Could *I have **some** water, please?*

You can also use *some* and *any* without a noun when you know what the person is talking about:

A: Is there any milk?

B: Yes, there is some in the fridge. (*some* = some milk)

A: Can I have an apple?

B: Sorry, but I don't have any. (*any* = any apples)

A Underline the correct word.

1. There are *some / any* vegetables in this bowl.

2. I don't have *some / any* fruit. Let's go to the store.

3. Does she have *some / any* water bottles?

4. They have *some / any* exams this week.

5. Can I have *some / any* chocolate cake?

6. The supermarket doesn't have *some / any* butter today.

7. Do you need *some / any* eggs?

8. There isn't *some / any* bread. Sorry!

B Write *some* or *any* to complete the conversation.

A: I'm going to the supermarket. Do we need (1) _____ meat?

B: No, we have (2) _____ in the fridge. It's chicken.

A: OK. What about vegetables? Do we have (3) _____?

B: We need (4) _____ potatoes. Oh, and can you get me (5) _____ bottles of water?

A: How many?

B: Six, please. Also, we don't have (6) _____ ice.

Lesson C

Count Nouns and Non-count Nouns	
Count Nouns (plural ending -*s*)	Non-count Nouns
Some nouns are countable. You can count them and they can become plural. They have a singular and plural form: *chair → chairs, carrot → carrots, pen → pens*	Other nouns are non-count. You cannot count them, and they are always singular: *rice, water, information*
Count nouns take singular and plural verbs: *The apple is red. The apples are red.*	Non-count nouns only take a singular verb: *The water is hot.*

C Check (✓) *count* or *non-count* for the nouns.

	Count	Non-count
1. time		✓
2. house		
3. book		
4. ice		
5. car		
6. key		
7. water		
8. salt		
9. train		
10. coffee		

How many / How much

How many + Count Nouns	How much + Non-count Nouns
We use *how many* to ask about plural count nouns: **How many trains** *are there to London today?*	We use *how much* to ask about non-count nouns: **How much coffee** *do you want?*

*We use *how much / how many* to ask about quantities.

D Write *many* or *much* to complete the conversation.

A: How (1) _____ people are coming?

B: Twenty, I think.

A: Do we have everything? How (2) _____ soda is there?

B: Ten bottles, so that's fine. Don't worry!

A: I'm not! How (3) _____ sandwiches are there?

B: About one hundred!

A: Wow! How (4) _____ money are we spending on this party?!

E Write the question for each answer. Start each question with *How much* or *How many*.

1. *How many boxes of chocolates are there* _____?

There are three boxes of chocolates.

2. _____?

Not much! I can buy some more pasta.

3. _____?

I have three brothers.

4. _____?

We only have one bottle, so can you buy some more orange juice?

5. _____?

I have three friends in my class.

UNIT 10

Lesson A

Feel, Look + Adjective

We use an adjective after the verbs *look* and *feel*:
*You look **great**!*
*They feel **terrible**!*

We often use these adjectives after *look* and *feel*: *great, happy, fantastic, OK, well / not well, terrible, sick, tired*

Affirmative and Negative

I / You / We / They	feel / don't feel look / don't look	well. tired.
He / She / It	feels / doesn't feel looks / doesn't look	sick. happy.

Yes / No Questions

Do	I / you / we / they	**feel**	tired?
Does	he / she / it	**look**	happy?

Short Answers

Yes, I **do**.	No, you **don't**.
Yes, he **does**.	No, she **doesn't**.

Information Questions

How do you **feel**?	Fine, thanks.
How is he **feeling**?	He's fine.

*You can ask these questions with no difference in meaning: *How do you feel? / How are you feeling?*

A Match the two halves of the sentences.

1. The two brothers feel _____

2. Do you _____

3. Sasha doesn't _____

4. You _____

5. How are _____

6. How do _____

7. Does _____

a. feel well.

b. you feel?

c. she look tired?

d. don't look well.

e. feel OK?

f. you feeling?

g. sick.

B Complete the sentences.

1. A: Do you feel OK?

   B: Yes, I _____.

2. A: How is Melanie?

   B: She doesn't _____ well.

3. A: How _____?

   B: I feel terrible.

4. A: What's the matter?

   B: I don't _____ well.

Lesson C

Should (for advice)

Affirmative and Negative

| I / You / He / She / It / We / They | **should** | take the medicine. |
| | **shouldn't** | go to work today. |

*We use *should* / *shouldn't* to ask for and give advice.
**Should* is a modal verb.
- It has no third-person *-s* with *he* / *she* / *it*: *He should go.* ~~He shoulds go.~~
- Don't use the auxiliary *do* with *should*: *You shouldn't go.* ~~You don't should go.~~
- Don't use *to* before the next verb: *You should go.* ~~You should to go.~~

Yes / No Questions	Short Answers
Should I go to bed?	Yes, you **should**. / No, you **shouldn't**.

Wh- Questions

What **should** I do?
Where **should** I go?

C Match the questions and answers.

1. I feel sick. Should I see a doctor? _____
2. I have a headache. What should I do? _____
3. Nelson has a toothache. What should he do? _____
4. Should Uzra see a doctor? _____
5. Hilary has a cough. What should she do? _____

a. You should take some pain relievers.
b. He should see a dentist.
c. She should take some cough medicine.
d. Yes, you should.
e. No, she shouldn't.

D Write *should* or *shouldn't* to complete the advice.

1. You look tired. You _____ go back to bed.
2. He has a bad toothache, so he _____ go to the dentist.
3. Sally has a fever, so she _____ go to school today.
4. My headache is terrible. I _____ take more pain relievers.

E Circle the mistake in each sentence and rewrite it.

1. You should to see the doctor.
   You should see the doctor.

2. We don't should eat junk food.
   _____

3. Bill shoulds go to bed.
   _____

4. Do I should take this medicine?
   _____

5. No, you don't should.
   _____

UNIT 11

Lesson A

Be going to

Statements

I	am 'm		
He She It	is 's	**going to**	go out for dinner. have a barbecue. go to the movies.
You We They	are 're		

*Use *be going to* to talk about making plans.
*We often use *be going to* with these time expressions: *tomorrow*, *next Sunday* / *week* / *year*.

Negatives

I	am not 'm not		
He She It	is not isn't	**going to**	have a party. meet my friends. celebrate the anniversary.
You We They	are not aren't		

Yes / No Questions				Short Answers
Are	you	**going**	have a	Yes, I **am**. / No, I'**m not**.
Is	he	**to**	party?	Yes, he **is**. / No, he **isn't**.

Wh- Questions

What are you **going to** do tomorrow?
Where are you **going to** celebrate?

A Match the questions to the answers.

1. Where are they going to live? _____
2. Is she going to come tonight? _____
3. Why are they going to have a party? _____
4. Are Miles and Irina going to get new jobs? _____
5. Are you going to take a vacation? _____

a. No, I'm not. Not this year.

b. Yes, she is.

c. Because it's their anniversary.

d. In a house near Monterrey.

e. Yes, they are.

B Complete the sentences using *be going to* and the verb.

1. I ___'m going to learn___ (learn) a new language.

2. You _____ (buy) some new clothes.

3. Ella _____ (meet) Ken at the cafe.

4. They _____ (not celebrate) her birthday.

5. He _____ (not go) to college.

6. _____ he _____ (have) a party?

7. What _____ you _____ (do)?

8. _____ we _____ (take) the bus?

Lesson C

Would like to for Wishes

Affirmative and Negative			
I / You / He / She / It / We / They	**would / 'd**	**like to**	study English in college.
	wouldn't		

*We use *would like to* to talk about wishes for the future.
*In everyday English, we contract *would*: *I'd like to study English.*
*Would is a modal verb.
  - It has no third-person *-s* with he / she / it: *He would like... / He woulds like...*.
  - Don't use the auxiliary *do* with *would*: *You wouldn't like. / You don't would like.*

Yes / No Questions	Short Answers
Would you **like to** be a teacher?	Yes, I **would**. / No, I **wouldn't**.

Wh- Questions	Answers
What **would** you **like to** do next? Where **would** you **like to** go?	I'**d like to** play soccer. I'**d like to** go to the movies.

C Unscramble the words.

1. to be / a / would / like / I / musician.

_____

2. Helen / like / What / would / to be?

_____

3. to be / Would / you / a / doctor? / like

_____

4. Deng / medicine. / would / to / study / like

_____

5. What / like / to be? / would / you

_____

D Write *would* or *wouldn't* to complete the conversation.

A: What (1) _____ you like to do when you leave school?

B: I'm going to travel for a year, then go to college.

A: That's interesting. (2) _____ you like to go around the world?

B: No, I (3) _____. I (4) _____ like to spend a long time in one country and learn about it.

E Circle the mistake in each sentence and rewrite it.

1. She woulds like to have a party.

_____

2. We don't would like to see that movie.

_____

3. I would to like to go out this evening.

_____

4. Do you would like to come to my birthday?

_____

UNIT 12

Lesson A

Simple Past

Statements		
I / You / He / She / It / We / They	**lived** **moved** **went** **left**	in London in 2000. to Lima last month. to the movies yesterday. school three years ago.

*Use the simple past to talk about completed actions and events in the past.
*Verbs in the simple past have one form: *I lived, you lived, he lived, she lived*

Regular Verbs

Spelling rules for regular verbs in the simple past:
  - Add *-ed* to most verbs ending with a consonant: *worked, stayed, started*
  - Change *y* to *i* with two-syllable verbs ending in *y*: *study → studied*

- Add -d to verbs ending in e: live → lived, move → moved
- Double the final letter with some verbs ending in a vowel + consonant: stop → stopped

Irregular Verbs

Some verbs are irregular. Do not add -ed in the simple past. Irregular verbs include:

buy – bought	do – did	drive – drove
eat – ate	get – got	give – gave
go – went	have – had	leave – left
make – made	meet – met	see – saw
sell – sold	take – took	wear – wore

Negatives

I / You / He / She / It / We / They	didn't	**live**	in London in 2000.
		move	to Lima last month.
		go	to the movies yesterday.
		leave	school two years ago.

*Use didn't for negative sentences in the simple past.

Was / were

The verb to be is irregular in the simple past.

I / He / She / It	**was**	born in 1966.
You / We / They	**were**	a doctor / doctors.

Negative		
I / He / She / It	**wasn't**	born in 1966.
You / We / They	**weren't**	a doctor / doctors.

A Change the sentences to the simple past.

1. I live in Amsterdam.
   I lived in Amsterdam.

2. They arrive at 10.
   _____

3. I go to my English class.
   _____

4. He is a teacher.
   _____

5. She studies mathematics.
   _____

6. We don't travel by train to Paris.
   _____

7. I buy my clothes at that shop.
   _____

8. My friends and I aren't busy.
   _____

9. This computer doesn't work.
   _____

10. Pamela and Mike don't like my cooking.
    _____

B Correct the spelling mistakes in these regular verbs.

1. studied ____studied____
2. stoped _____
3. visitied _____
4. liveed _____
5. moveed _____

C Complete this table of irregular verbs.

Present	Past
1. sell	_____
2. _____	took
3. has	_____
4. go	_____
5. _____	got
6. _____	did

Cardinal Numbers	Ordinal Numbers
1 one	1st first
2 two	2nd second
3 three	3rd third
4 four	4th fourth
5 five	5th fifth
6 six	6th sixth
7 seven	7th seventh
8 eight	8th eighth
9 nine	9th ninth
10 ten	10th tenth
11 eleven	11th eleventh
20 twenty	20th twentieth
21 twenty-one	21st twenty-first
22 twenty-two	22nd twenty-second

Lesson B

Simple Past Questions

Was / Were Questions		
Was	I / he / she / it	a student / students?
Were	you / we / they	

Short Answers		
Yes,	I / he / she / it	**was**.
	you / we / they	**were**.
No,	I / he / she / it	**wasn't**.
	you / we / they	**weren't**.

Wh- Questions	
What did you do?	I went to the movies.
When were you born?	In 2001.
Where did you live?	I lived in California.
How long did you study there?	I studied for 3 years.

D Unscramble the words.

1. arrive at / when / did you / school / ?

   _____

2. home / you / did / leave / why / ?

   _____

3. your friends / at / were / the cafe / ?

   _____

4. in / did / how long / you live / Bangkok / ?

   _____

5. did / work / they / where / ?

   _____

6. Michael / the party / was / at ?

   _____

E Write the missing words to complete the conversation.

A: (1) _____*Were*_____ you born in Canada?

B: No, I (2) _____. I (3) _____ born in Syria, but my parents moved to France.

A: How long (4) _____ you stay in France?

B: Twelve years. But then I left France when I (5) _____ 18 to study in the US.

A: (6) _____ did you come to Canada?

B: I (7) _____ about five years ago.

Lesson C

Yes / No Questions				
Did	I / you / he / she / it / we / they	**go**	to college?
Short Answers				
Yes,	I / he / she / it / you / we / they	**did**.
No,	I / he / she / it / you / we / they	**didn't**.

F Complete the questions and answers with *did* or *didn't*.

1. **A:** _____ they have a goodbye party?
   B: Yes, they _____. It was fun!

2. **A:** _____ you sell the house?
   B: No, we _____.

3. **A:** _____ Ian buy the tickets?
   B: Yes, he _____. Well, he bought the train tickets, but he _____ buy the bus tickets.

4. **A:** _____ she get a visa?
   B: No, she _____. She _____ need one.

Common Irregular Verbs

Base Form	Simple Past	Past Participle	Base Form	Simple Past	Past Participle
begin	began	begun	make	made	made
break	broke	broken	meet	met	met
bring	brought	brought	pay	paid	paid
buy	bought	bought	put	put	put
come	came	come	read	read	read
do	did	done	ride	rode	ridden
drink	drank	drunk	run	ran	run
drive	drove	driven	say	said	said
eat	ate	eaten	see	saw	seen
feel	felt	felt	send	sent	sent
get	got	gotten	sit	sat	sat
give	gave	given	sleep	slept	slept
go	went	gone	speak	spoke	spoken
have	had	had	swim	swam	swum
hear	heard	heard	take	took	taken
hurt	hurt	hurt	tell	told	told
know	knew	known	think	thought	thought
leave	left	left	throw	threw	thrown
let	let	let	understand	understood	understood
lose	lost	lost	write	wrote	written

Credits

COVER

Inge Johnsson/Alamy Stock Photo.

ILLUSTRATIONS

All Illustrations are owned by © Cengage.

iv (tl1) Martin Schoeller/National Geographic Image Collection; (tl2) © Gabriel Galimberti/Institute; (cl1) © Peter Stewart; (cl2) © Chelsea Nix; (bl1) © Michael Vong; (bl2) © Rogerio Reis/TYBA; **vi** (tl1) Yuri Kozyrev/Noor/Redux; (tl2) © Chris Saunders/Lampost; (cl1) © Mieko Horikoshi; (cl2) © Wagner Araujo; (bl1) Muhammed Muheisen/National Geographic Image Collection; (bl2) Evgenia Arbugaeva/National Geographic Image Collection; **2** Martin Schoeller/National Geographic Image Collection; **3** (tl) (tr) (bl) Martin Schoeller/National Geographic Image Collection; **4** (tl) South_agency/E+/Getty Images; (tr) PeopleImages/E+/Getty Images; (cl) laflor/E+/Getty Images; (cr) Klaus Vedfelt/Iconica/Getty Images; **6** Hufton+Crow/View Pictures/Contributor/Universal Images Group/Getty Images; **8** (tl) Novastock/Photolibrary/Getty Images; (tc1) thebang/Moment/Getty Images; (tc2) Halfpoint/iStock/Getty Images; (tr) PeopleImages/E+/Getty Images; (cl1) Maskot/DigitalVision/Getty Images; (cl2) MStudioImages/E+/Getty Images; (cl3) Poike/iStock/Getty Images; (bl1) andresr/E+/Getty Images; (bl2) Cheryl Savan/Shutterstock.com; **10–11** (spread) Dr. Mary Droser/National Geographic Image Collection; **12** (c) (cr) AJR_photo/Shutterstock.com; **15** Markus Hintzen/laif/Redux; **16–17** (spread) © Gabriel Galimberti/Institute; **18** (tl1) The Num Phanu Studio/Shutterstock.com; (tc1) Kyle Monk/Blend Images/Getty Images; (tc2) Ryan McVay/The Image Bank/Getty Images; (tr1) Raphye Alexius/Image Source/Getty Images; (tl2) DCPhoto/Alamy Stock Photo; (tc3) Jose Luis Pelaez Inc/DigitalVision/Getty Images; (tc4) skynesher/E+/Getty Images; (tr2) Compassionate Eye Foundation/Karan Kapoor/DigitalVision/Getty Images; **20** (tl) © GuelphToday; (tr) South China Morning Post/Contributor/Getty Images; **22** National Geographic Maps; **24–25** (spread) © Alison Wright Photography; **26** (cr) Scott Dickerson/Design Pics/First Light/Getty Images; (b) Steve Woods Photography/Cultura/Getty Images; **28** (t) Alain Lauga/Shutterstock.com; **28–29** (spread) © Yoshiyuki "Okotanpe" Fuse; **30–31** (spread) © Peter Stewart; **34** (tl) © Teo Han Yang Effendi Jeremy; (tr) © Oscar Ruiz Cardeña; **35** (c) David Santiago Garcia/Aurora/Getty Images; (b) Marko Djurica/Reuters; **36** (tl1) Gamaruba/Shutterstock.com; (tl2) Photobac/Shutterstock.com; (tc1) Ruslan Ivantsov/Shutterstock.com; (tr1) Sandratsky Dmitriy/Shutterstock.com; (tr2) Pix11/Shutterstock.com; (tl3) Perla Berant Wilder/Shutterstock.com; (tc2) Carlos Amarillo/Shutterstock.com; (tr3) Pix11/Shutterstock.com; (tr4) mbbirdy/E+/Getty Images; (tr5) ParvinMaharramov/Shutterstock.com; (cl) Protasov AN/Shutterstock.com; (c1) Zovteva/Shutterstock.com; (c2) HappyAprilBoy/Shutterstock.com; (cr) John Kasawa/Shutterstock.com; **37** FluxFactory/E+/Getty Images; **38–39** (spread) © Nadia Drake; **41** View Pictures/Contributor/Universal Images Group/Getty Images; **42–43** (spread) © Jon Arnold/Danita Delimont Stock Photography; **44–45** (spread) © Chelsea Nix; **46** (tl) Shell114/Deposit Photos; (tc1) Nattstudio/Shutterstock.com; (tc2) Becky Starsmore/

Shutterstock.com; (tr) Jo Ann Snover/Shutterstock.com; (cl1) bondarchuk/Shutterstock.com; (c1) Sergiy Kuzmin/Shutterstock.com; (c2) Andrew Buckin/Shutterstock.com; (cr1) Sangaroon/Shutterstock.com; (cl2) Karlis Dambrans/Shutterstock.com; (c3) Jin young-in/Shutterstock.com; (c4) eldadcarin/iStock Editorial/Getty Images; (cr2) krungchingpixs/iStock/Getty Images; **48** © Hetain Patel; **50** (tl1) Louis Turner/Cultura/Getty Images; (tl2) JZhuk/iStock/Getty Images; (tc) Album/Alamy Stock Photo; **52–53** (spread) © John Thackwray; **54** JGalione/E+/Getty Images; **56** (t) Jon Bowen/National Geographic Image Collection; **56–57** (spread) © Tyler Metcalfe; **58–59** (spread) © Michael Vong; **60** (tl1) torwai/iStock/Getty Images; (tl2) imtmphoto/Shutterstock.com; (tc1) Nattharit Poungpath/EyeEm/Getty Images; (tr1) Tetra Images/Brand X Pictures/Getty Images; (tr2) sturti/E+/Getty Images; (tl3) Thomas Barwick/Stone/Getty Images; (tl4) Jonathan Knowles/The Image Bank/Getty Images; (tc2) Muslim Girl/DigitalVision/Getty Images; (tr3) Tanya Yatsenko/Shutterstock.com; (tr4) Oleksandr Nagaiets/Alamy Stock Photo; **62** Carolyn Drake/Magnum Photos; **64** (tl1) Rawpixel.com/Shutterstock.com; (tc1) Troy Aossey/Taxi/Getty Images; (tc2) Reza Estakhrian/Stone/Getty Images; (tr1) Shine Nucha/Shutterstock.com; (tl2) hobo_018/E+/Getty Images; (tc3) Alain Le Bot/Photononstop/Getty Images; (tc4) Caiaimage/Sam Edwards/Getty Images; (tr2) monkeybusinessimages/iStock/Getty Images; **66–67** (spread) John Stanmeyer/National Geographic Image Collection; **68** Magnus Wennman/National Geographical Image Collection; **70–71** (spread) Cody Duncan/Age Fotostock/Media Bakery; **72–73** (spread) © Rogerio Reis/TYBA; **76** (t) BrazilPhotos/Alamy Stock Photo; (b) National Geographic Maps; **78** (tc) Vladislav Sinelnikov/Shutterstock.com; (tr) Jeff Greenberg/Contributor/Universal Images Group/Getty Images; (cl) Rainer Grosskopf/Photolibrary/Getty Images; (c) Jeff Greenberg/Contributor/Universal Images Group/Getty Images; (cr) Jose A Feliciano Cestero/iStock/Getty Images; **80–81** (spread) Fotos593/Shutterstock.com; **83** Alexander Spatari/Moment/Getty Images; **84–85** (spread) © Improv Everywhere Productions, Inc.; **86–87** (spread) Yuri Kozyrev/Noor/Redux; **88** (tl1) AP Images/Ng Han Guan; (tc1) Leren Lu/Taxi Japan/Getty Images; (tc2) damircudic/E+/Getty Images; (tr1) andresr/E+/Getty Images; (tl2) Trevor Williams/DigitalVision/Getty Images; (tc3) martin-dm/E+/Getty Images; (tc4) PeopleImages/E+/Getty Images; (tr2) Thomas Barwick/DigitalVision/Getty Images; **90** (tl) Images Bazaar/Brand Images Plus/Getty Images; (tc) Image Source/DigitalVision/Getty Images; (tr) Cultura Creative (RF)/Alamy Stock Photo; **92** (tl1) Microgen/Shutterstock.com; (tc1) Cavan Images/Getty Images; (tc2) dotshock/Shutterstock.com; (tr1) lzf/Shutterstock.com; (tl2) Caroline von Tuempling/Iconica/Getty Images; (tc3) Jordan Siemens/Iconica/Getty Images; (tc4) FatCamera/E+/Getty Images; (tr2) Lukas Gojda/Shutterstock.com; **94–95** (spread) Jaap Arriens/ZUMA Press/Newscom; **96** Andreas Hub/laif/Redux; **98–99** (spread) Harry Borden/Contributor/Contour/Getty Images; **100–101** (spread) © Chris Saunders/Lampost; **102** (tl) xiaorui/Shutterstock.com; (tc1) Vlad Teodor/Shutterstock.com; (tc2) donikz/Shutterstock.com; (tr) Elnur/Shutterstock.com; (cl1) Nattika/Shutterstock.com; (cl2) Irina Rogova/Shutterstock.com; (c1) Michael Kraus/Shutterstock.com; (c2) KoBoZaa/Shutterstock.com; (cr1) CapturePB/Shutterstock.com; (cl3) Tarzhanova/

iStock/Getty Images; (cl4) New Africa/Shutterstock.com; (c3) Karkas/Shutterstock.com; (c4) GaryAlvis/E+/Getty Images; (cr2) FeellFree/Shutterstock.com; **104** Mark Mawson/Stone/Getty Images; **106** JeffG/Alamy Stock Photo; **108–109** (spread) Portra/DigitalVision/Getty Images; **111** pranodhm/iStock/Getty Images; **112–113** (spread) © Andrea Pecora; **114–115** (spread) © Mieko Horikoshi; **116** (tl) Linda Studley/Shutterstock.com; (tc1) siambizkit/Shutterstock.com; (tc2) Davidchuk Alexey/Shutterstock.com; (tr) Tatiana Volgutova/Shutterstock.com; (cl1) Elenadesign/Shutterstock.com; (c1) Foodio/Shutterstock.com; (c2) liv friis-larsen/Alamy Stock Photo; (cr1) bitt24/Shutterstock.com; (cl2) Jerry Lin/Shutterstock.com; (c3) Sofiaworld/Shutterstock.com; (c4) helen bird/Shutterstock.com; (cr2) GMVozd/E+/Getty Images; **118** (t) AdShooter/E+/Getty Images; **122–123** (spread) Brian Finke/National Geographic Image Collection; **124–125** (spread) Robert Clark/National Geographic Image Collection; **126–127** (spread) dpa picture alliance archive/Alamy Stock Photo; **128–129** (spread) © Wagner Araujo; **130** John Stanmeyer/National Geographic Image Collection; **134** (tl1) Hero Images Inc./Alamy Stock Photo; (tc1) Helen Ashford/Stone/Getty Images; (tr1) Tetra Images/Getty Images; (tl2) Fred Tanneau/AFP/Stringer/Getty Images; (tc2) Sujata Jana/EyeEm/Getty Images; (tr2) Rekinc1980/E+/Getty Images; **136–137** (spread) © Stephen Shankland/CNET; **138** Glogowsk/LAIF/Redux; **140–141** (spread) © James Kaiser; **142–143** (spread) Muhammed Muheisen/National Geographic Image Collection; **144** (tl1) ZUMA/ZUMA Wire Service/Alamy Stock Photo; (tc1) Jurij Krupiak/Shutterstock.com; (tr1) fizkes/iStock/Getty Images; (tl2) VGstockstudio/Shutterstock.com; (tc2) Pollyana Ventura/E+/Getty Images; (tr2) RubberBall Productions/Brand X Pictures/Getty Images; **146** (tl) AP Images/John Minchillo; (tr) Andre Vogelaere/Moment/Getty Images; **148** (t) © Emilia Wilgosz-Peter; (bl1) Hero Images/Getty Images; (bc1) Aleksandar Karanov/Shutterstock.com; (br1) Michael Staudt/VISUM/Redux; (bl2) Peter Essick/Aurora Photos; (bc2) metamorworks/Shutterstock.com; (br2) Klaus Vedfelt/DigitalVision/Getty Images; **150–151** (spread) Daniel Ochoa De Olza/National Geographic Image Collection; **151** (cr) 7maru/iStock Editorial/Getty Images; (br) Poras Chaudhary/Stone/Getty Images; **152** Marc Bruxelle/Alamy Stock Photo; **154–155** (spread) Anand Varma/National Geographic Image Collection; **156–157** (spread) Evgenia Arbugaeva/National Geographic Image Collection; **158** (tl1) James Andrews/iStock/Getty Images; (tc1) Monkey Business Images/Shutterstock.com; (tr1) valentinrussanov/E+/Getty Images; (tl2) VStock/Alamy Stock Photo; (tc2) Blue Jean Images/Alamy Stock Photo; (tr2) Alvey & Towers Picture Library/Alamy Stock Photo; (cl) Dragon Images/Shutterstock.com; (c) fizkes/Shutterstock.com; (cr) Monkey Business Images/Shutterstock.com; **160** Chris Thornton/National Geographic Image Collection; **162** (tl1) PhotoTalk/E+/Getty Images; (tc1) igor kisselev/Alamy Stock Photo; (tc2) JeffG/Alamy Stock Photo; (tr1) Aja Koska/E+/Getty Images; (tl2) sebra/Shutterstock.com; (tc3) © Chuck Haney/Danita Delimont Stock Photography; (tc4) svetikd/E+/Getty Images; (tr2) guruXOX/Shutterstock.com; **164–165** (spread) Steve Winter/National Geographic Image Collection; **167** Nasa; **168–169** (spread) Paul Nicklen/National Geographic Image Collection.